ARNA

THE JOURNAL OF THE

UNIVERSITY OF SYDNEY ARTS STUDENTS' SOCIETY

2013

First published 2013 by Darlington Press
Funded by The University of Sydney Union
and The University of Sydney Faculty of Arts

Images have been used in this book. Every effort has been made
to identify and attribute credit appropriately. The editors thank
contributors for permission to reproduce their work.

ISBN 978-1-921364-50-1

Fisher Library F03
University of Sydney
NSW 2006 Australia
Email: sup.info@sydney.edu.au
Web: sydney.edu.au/sup

Cover photo by Katherine Johns

ARNA is brought to you by

Editors-in-chief	Alberta McKenzie
	Lane Sainty
General & critical editors	Nicholas Fahy
	Madeleine Konstantinidis
Creative editors	Georgia Behrens
	Katie Davern
	Shirley Huang
	Ashleigh Maihi
	Mira Schlosberg
Poetry editors	Finn Gabriel Keogh
	Celeste Moore
	Gila Segall
	Varsha Srinivasan
Visual editors	Phoebe Johnson
	Freia Kirkaldy
	Gillian Watt
First-year editors	Jessica Cheng
	Whitney Duan
	Grace Lovell-Davis
	Jack Wells
	Darren Zeng
Designer	Julia Zhu Wei

Thanks to

The University of Sydney Union
The University of Sydney Arts Students' Society
The Faculty of Arts and Social Sciences
Agata Mrva-Montoya
Bronwyn O'Reilly
Alex McKinnon
Eden Tollis

Contents

Foreword

Alberta McKenzie and Lane Sainty

The eight-month long haul placing this book in your palms is a story of pride, of the buoyant creative community at the University of Sydney and, frankly, includes a lengthy personal ramble from the editors and executive members of the Sydney Arts Students' Society.

Ain't nobody got time for that – especially you, because after you read this, you have pages of literary deliciousness to devour.

Instead, we wish to use this foreword to remind people to stop just once in a while. Contrary to popular belief, arts students do not possess infinite amounts of spare time. The rush of submissions we received just prior to the deadline is indicative of this. Our lives are dictated by our proclivity to over-committing; we live from deadline to deadline, filling the time in between with periods of procrastination punctuated by those of extreme stress.

This life is not unpleasant, nor is it unfulfilling. But it often prioritises that which is necessary for survival, in life or degree, over that which is enjoyable. Too often, we are less inclined to make time for the creative arts.

We hope that this journal represents a connection to that time when you had time – without, of course, being a relic of the past. We hope it serves not as a reminder of the books piled high upon your bedside table, but as a validation that you can find time to read them all.

Many of the submissions for ARNA 2013 made us stop in our tracks. Engrossed in a compelling description of city life, struck by the beauty of a delicate phrase in a poem, or taken aback by the dedicated pursuit of the perfect word undertaken by our contributors during the editing period, at many points we paused and considered the talents of our peers.

It has been our honour to collate the fine work of so many University of Sydney students into this humble journal. We sincerely hope you take some time to consume it. Read it slowly. Revel in the talents of your friends. Appreciate its tangibility.

Heartbreak Hotel

Joel Mak

Oui oui, Heartbreak Hotel. The Heartbreak Hotel. Est. circa 1956 and 1956 being of course the year Elvis, the one and only King, released the eponymous song. Now, of course the concept of it predated 1956: the King merely solidified its existence on the radio waves. That men everywhere have had to deal with quote unquote woman issues since time immemorial is indisputable. There is no doubt that every single one of our ancestors – yes, way back to Homo erectus – has had their heart broken by a woman (for whatever reason: rejection, divorce, misunderstandings, untimely death, etc.) at least once in their entire life; and that regardless of the context our subject male usually found himself at the Heartbreak Hotel.

These hotels, ubiquitous in both temporal and spatial dimensions, are always pointed out to you by the giant billboard off the shoulder of the freeway's exit; the poster's been there since 1956 too and you can't even make out the words but if you're potential clientele you darn well know what it's advertising for $99 a night. The buildings themselves are always single eight- to ten-storey blocks and from far you notice the sheets of paint flaking off the walls (salmon coloured in 1956 but now stained charcoal black as though it's been through a fire), the walls lighted by the hotel's neon sign flickering like a demented firefly.

In the interior on the ground floor there'd be a bar leading off from reception manned by the oldest person you've ever seen whose eyesight no prescription glasses will fix, bless him. The bar would be as dark as the ones in your standard Humphrey Bogart classic and the bald obese Hungarian wouldn't even have any ice to chill your warm insipid beer. The bar's carpet would be stained by god-knows-what such that its original bright red would be a messy burgundy and there'd be empty beer bottles scattered everywhere alongside overturned ashtrays covering their spilled contents, none of it being tidied up by any of the cleaning ladies since the Mesozoic era, so they now blend in as part of the ambiance and the decor. You can hear the whispered conversations over the haunting voice of Robert Johnson on the stereo, the men shrugging in solidarity like tired mobsters, most of them using uncouth epithets for their exes while they fling darts at enlarged photos of the women who once gave meaning to their lives. And of course, let's not even mention the happy hour which the bar never bothers hosting.

Re the cleaning ladies: they would be Latinas, none of them any good with English and the clientele would hardly see them anyway; though on the rare occasion that there is a face-à-face: they (the cleaning ladies) would look at the men with eyes that only Latinas are born with, eyes that you could talk all day long to; tender sympathetic eyes fixed on the men's empty glazed ones, while they'd ask the Latinas to excuse their inebriation but such inebriation was necessary because their woman done left them you understand?; the emerald irises conveying very clearly that no sé señor at all but full of South American compassion which would only make the lumps in the throats of these men ache a notch more than they had been since check-in.

The corridors in which the clientele and the cleaning ladies would have their infrequent meets would be long: the theory is complex but essentially one's room would be at the end of it and its length would be ten metres multiplied by the number of days one had been in the now finito relationship. The theory allows for men to occupy rooms between the lifts and their rooms even though they like everyone else were supposed to have their room right at the end of the corridor but to reiterate, it's complex and the mathematics of this are, even as we speak, being worked out by a doctoral student in joint mathematics and psychology.

None of these men have been primed to Let It Out. The fathers of these men and their fathers[1] have always equated crying, weeping, bawling, anything involving moisture in the

---

1   Again, way back to Homo erectus.

eyes, etc. to those fruit-tree-in-the-Garden-of-Eden situations where violating this simple principle, however tempting, would disrupt the equilibrium of things, warning them that proverbial shit awaited the man who dared cry first, quod vide the entire Bible after the first few chapters of Genesis. So Heartbreak Hotel's clientele would be in their individual rooms[2] either dancing the tango solo[3] or holding in their tears after they'd done the deed. So in essence there's this metaphorical and also physical humongous cloud hovering above and around the hotel bursting through the seams with precipitation but only ever eking a drop here and there. In other words: the place is as tense as the final minutes of each client's preferred reality-television game show.[4] One imagines a sop-fest of Niagara-Falls proportions the moment one man decides he cannot hold it in anymore and doesn't mind shaming an entire gender group and so finally Lets It All Out, triggering a falling domino chain of crying men from the end of the corridor down to the lifts, the crying contagious and spreading to the lower and upper floors and to the bar, men of generations past, present and future discharging enough water to revive the dry zones of South Australia.

Yet, to the men and women outside in the normal world, these unfamiliar sounds from crying men that would seep out in disjunctive waves via the revolving door would only be interpreted as the sounds of men having the time of their lives in what to them really only looks like a brothel.

2　Furnished with one single bed under which rats and roaches fornicate like one big happy family, one mounted cathode-ray television, one dresser, half-closed windows stuck due to the sedimentation of gum, mould and crud in the jambs overlooking the hotel's destitute vandalised car park, one shower cubicle with a slow-dripping shower head with a tattered note taped to its side 'PLUMBER ARRIVING TOMORROW', and one empty minibar.

3　The Heartbreak Hotel being the only hotel in the world whose guests click 'Buy' on the remotes aimed at the Adult Channels.

4　Popular shows of choice: *America's next top model*, *The voice*, *Survivor* and *The bachelor* (the last of these preferred to *The bachelorette*, for obvious reasons).

Meiosis – The Unidentical Daughter Cell

Deeba Binai

Aeroplanes thunder through their sky
and throttle the street.

The only stoic building is the whorehouse, one block down –
the unapologetic 'open' sign winking;
and pink panties flirting from behind the blinds.

Sun-dappled palm-frond sheets hang like broken fingers
from knuckles of watermelon-green stripes;
the way a raised hand is a predator.

Grunge and bass throb in a bowling alley next door –
a makeshift rave dropping thunder,
pounding storms wet, funky, and moulding.

The mulch in the backyard frames the shit grass and flaccid
rainforest
that refuses to dry, ambivalent in viscous humidity.

She's dividing herself, and dividing herself
in self defence –
              and it's like the oceans can't really separate
but she's pulling apart pomegranate pieces
              into dripping, uneven bits of fertile disappointment.

A Paean to Youth and Death in Three Parts

Charlie O'Grady

Living breathing house, filled with antiques and decorative, but
warm with candlelight and affection, warmer with bodies inside
– bursting with the heavy sighing pastiche of youthful nostalgia –
I pass a mask on the wall on the way in, watch its smooth white
face and vacant made-up eyes, a grown-up china doll child: I
look at it and see myself, nod in unspoken recognition, solidarity
in a disappearing identity.

I

There is a swaying in the air –
not that we ourselves sway,
but that the nothingness sways
dances
the world turns more like reckless
car rides in unknown territories
than the slow work of physics,
and we, powerless and hungry,
angry starry-eyed marionettes,
are moved by it.
There is a taste to the night
on the grooves of mouths, the
tips of tongues searching out
the skin of others, a taste of
newness in ancient ritual,
of Renewal fucking Nostalgia
in the full moon.

There is a peace in cacophony
A stillness in frenetic laziness
A constant wakeful sharpness
in drunken death slumber.
This room will not sleep, I think
This time we will be forever.

II

*I thought and thought until the insides of my eyelids were green
and the world around too too blue. I thought and thought in
circles and jagged patterns, closing my eyes to the rush of image
and sound and light and screaming silence and blackblackblack.
I chased fractures of burning, stark white light around the walls
of my skull, felt light bounce and bend around each one of my
fears, elongated shadows making them appear strange and small
– felt them crack and shatter and disintegrate with every blow. I
let it happen and happen until the dust and debris and residue
dripped warm from my ears down my neck staining my clothes
staining the sofa cushions burning dirty yellow holes in fabric
and skin; until my head felt empty, light, so light it wobbled on
my brittle neck and fell with hollow echoing thud on the floor;
until the breeze smoothed my features away like wind on sand
and I saw nothing heard nothing felt nothing but churn and
pound of thought. I thought and I thought until thought con-
sumed me, hours bled into days and years until I was nothing but
thought in purest form, free of doubt and unknown and broken,
nothing at all but the flow of thought, and it was the bare early
morning glow and I was immortal in mind.*

The imminence of loss has a gravity:
we ground ourselves to these
mad nights, these mad ones whose
lips form silent screams of laughter
in pictures and in memories forever

it is why we fight the wretched dawn
or the droop of our traitor eyelids.

There is messiness in the way we fight
and fuck and laugh and breathe
cry shout sing spit run exalt dance *howl*
and fall and drink in hot liquid death
 – arrogant vigilantes of the lines blurred
we wage wars with chaos our weapon
of choice, against the neatness of
ending, conclusion, destruction, death.

III

The room is dead now,
            sleeping,
       but silence tastes like just like death
               if your ears are still ringing.
         The mask on the wall becomes a face,
             a body – a beautiful woman
    holds out her hands to me and
asks to hold
        the weight of the globe slung across my shoulders;
    she holds it easily and
      spins it in one palm and
speaks softly,
       a voice defying cadence
         words gleaming in speech

    'stop leaving all the broken parts

    inside you'

so with pen in hand
sunset heart holding back night
with the scratch of ink on paper
ink on skin and skin on paper
with brandy warmth on tongue

dry enough to feel the annals of
history against teeth lips that
feel more like pages yet unwritten
than marked and marred flesh
I forget about Sleep and Thought
about Renewal and Nostalgia
still tight entangled in the corner
I throw my shoulder to the ending
with words and not insomnia
and I enjoy –

Letter to the Apocalypse

Phoebe Chen

Blue was orphaned in a storm. Dust clouds blinded him and tore him away from Mother Star's gentle orbit. It was only when he'd drifted far from the cosmic carnage that he looked back and saw how his ravaged home shone in bruised patches of purple and green.

He saw great stars die at a distance, flickering specks extinguished like faltering streetlights. He travelled through nebulas like the one that ejected him from his natal galaxy. He became an imprisoned wanderer, free to traverse the in-between worlds so long as he didn't become part of any system. He knew he was bound to some unknowable trajectory because he could never go in the directions he wanted to. Some light years ago, he had drifted by a star cluster, a scintillating symposium of the young and old, and wanted to join them. A few billion years passed and the intergalactic solitude bred bitterness in his middle age.

* * *

I imagine it would be lonely in deep space, where thoughts echo ad infinitum and nothing can respond. If there was any capacity for sound in space, it should be filled with a string symphony or Daft Punk. Panoramic pathos or cosmic rave.

* * *

When Diana Lindberg's father found out he was going to die before Earth collided with one rogue blue planet, he'd requested that they play Holst's *The planets* suite at his funeral. He thought it would be funny at the conclusion of his existence to remind everyone else about the imminent conclusions of their own. It was two weeks, three days and four hours from D-day/the Second Coming when the stroke took him, and later Diana sat next to me in her car not knowing if there was any point in burying a dead man on a soon-to-be dead planet. We were drinking coffee from the small stand in the hospital car park because the vendor didn't seem to believe that an Earth-bound projectile was any reason to stop working. Diana wanted to ask him how he could carry on like that, how the news hadn't severed these quotidian rites. 'Have you noticed how everything seems so much slower?' she said. Through her eyes, the city had fallen into a drugged reverie, its former dynamism poisoned by tranquiliser.

'Even the lights are slower now, don't you think?' she said later as we reached the intersection of the main road and Westlake Park. Traffic lights seemed less responsive, neon signs flashed with long pauses in-between.

Her father hadn't seemed to mind impending obliteration, not even when his health was somewhat steady. 'Everything comes and goes,' he used to say, 'The sooner you get your head around that, the less anxious you'll be about all of this.'

I remember when he used to be a university lecturer, trumpeting this strange ethos as his students watched their maverick professor dismiss half the Western literary canon. Some of them didn't understand him, didn't see how time had rendered supposedly transcendent stories obsolete. Everything comes and goes. Diana said that when she'd asked him about his own academic legacy, he seemed genuinely dismissive. Don't you want people to cite your work in their dissertations, to immortalise your ideas in nationally televised debates? He replied that immortality of anything as abstract would be particularly irrelevant to him when he was dead and buried. Worrying is the domain of the living; worries about work for posterity and coffee stand profits have no place in a subterranean necropolis.

* * *

Blue reached our galaxy when he passed through Westerlund 1, the super cluster of young, vivacious stars packed into one tight patch of space. He thought maybe his loneliness would abandon him, a detachable appendage that would vanish into the vast nothing, but as he wove in and out between these burning stars, he felt his loneliness multiply. It was like the disconnect in overflowing clubs, bumping hips and elbows with strangers and spilling drinks on expensive dresses without ever caring who they might belong to. Sometimes the stars would scorch his sides, but Blue couldn't hit them back.

* * *

Diana entertained the idea of cremation, incinerating sixty-five years of paternal love and blood and reducing it to a little box of ashes. But they couldn't have a funeral with that, not with a container the size of a book. If there was to be pomp and circumstance, she wanted the body there in its entirety, every clogged artery and sun spot.

'No, we can't just cremate him,' she said abruptly. 'I think I need a proper funeral because I don't want people to forget about him.' She needed new memories to float about in other people's heads so they could pass thoughts around like a mystical torch commemorating the great Professor Lindberg. She knew he didn't care, but it wasn't about him anymore.

We turned the corner onto Gabardine Road, where the edge of the park met the urban cement. Tall elms overlooked the bordering footpath frequented by joggers in summer, a momentary shadowed reprieve from the adjacent sun-scorched pavement. The stillness was strange, as though one morning, the city had simply swallowed the spandex-clad minority.

The car jilted suddenly, its front wheels caught on a slight hitch. I looked out the window and couldn't see a thing. Diana craned her neck and reversed a few metres.

'Oh.'

A cluster of contorted fur lay pressed against the gravel, tail twitching erratically. Diana leapt out of the car and knelt on the road.

'It's a cat,' she shouted over the engine. 'I think it's still alive.'

Its movements were barely perceptible, but its yellow eyes remained wide in a frenzy it could not otherwise express. It was beyond whimpering mews, deprived even of its feline language by a splintered bone here, a crushed vocal cord there. We stayed on the road until its bright eyes saw death and ceased their frantic darting. Diana stroked its damp fur. 'It's quite fat.'

She was right; its belly hung halfway to its paws, oddly disproportionate to its torso. She pressed its swollen stomach. 'Or maybe it was pregnant. I've run over a pregnant cat.'

We moved the gravel-splintered body onto the pedestrian path, at the foot of a towering elm tree. Diana rearranged its limbs and lifted its limp head against the trunk. I could see some subconscious symbolism surfacing in her mind, alloying the bark-blanketed roots with rebirth and life; the fat cat's spirit reincarnated in a leaf on the tree. She pulled a few ornamental weeds from the park grounds and lay them on the cat's head, which had a more comical effect than she'd anticipated.

She turned to me and began to cry, quietly at first, then hysterically, a torrential tempest asking *why*, not about the cat, not why it was pregnant or why she had flattened it into road kill, not why she'd sent it into its afterlife with weeds on its head. Not the cat; nothing about the cat. She wanted to know why Blue's fate was so interminably bound with ours, because she wanted the cat to live, even as a spirit in the leaf of a tree, and for her father's memory to haunt the annals of academia.

And so I told her to think about it like this, that Blue had lived to middle age with nothing and no one. That the lonely planet had drifted in a boundless vacuum and watched worlds be birthed and falter as a spectator on the sidelines, and not once had he really been part of anything, not since he was so very, very young back in his natal galaxy. Now, he was wandering towards us not with malicious intent, but with the same resignation and horror that we projected to him. 'So don't blame him', I said. 'He doesn't want to burn on impact and fall to pieces either. It's just something that's going to happen'.

His Winter Jacket

Mariana Podesta-Diverio

Thump.
Ka-thump.
It is of birth to saunter,
of naiveté to trust.
Square boxes left atop
birch perches announce
their bellowed presence to the rainiest world.
'Here am I,' call a dozen water droplets
from each soggy
box's corner.
Thump.

Thump.
Ka-thump.
A reformer's brainy foe is made of dried cedar.
Corona radiata: nature's misplaced call
to stately branches
that bear in mind the
deadly fall.
Leaves
that
mind the step
when entering seasons.

An autumn yard, for unknown reasons, kept
his winter jacket clung with beaming earnest solitude
to faded chair (once sea-green, to be fair).
Unwittingly, his laughter
yielded prime poetic
magnitude.

His
speech –
absent of debt,
devoid of treason,
danced a gruff line across dark den.
'Again, do tell me how it happened.'
Worn and torn from repetition, but I cared not.
Renditions mattered only when I whispered them to him:
'I was young and running. The wall came out of nowhere.'

Like this poem, if looked at sideways, the scar almost looks like
a tiny heartbeat segment peaking at the end of this line with a
disarming 'I feel so alive!'
Yet crescendo stings like wall-smack when crudely indicated
and foreheads don't make adequate hospital screens.

So, slow grins spread across faces if places of worship
that are only for us leave spaces for loud racket.
The coldest, drollest, best occasions
for his winter jacket.
Ka-thump.
Thump.

Exposure

Oscar Monaghan

It doesn't take much for scents to mingle:
spilled wine from a knocked glass is
spilled wine from a hundred glasses.

The smell, an envelope of sensation.
my body has not learnt to distinguish
the now
from before.

We hold memories under our skin, stretched taut and
porously thin, over muscles and nerves that learnt how
to be muscles and nerves behind bedroom doors, on the
other side of campervan walls.

Muscles that find memories of tightness in tensed calves, clenched
fists: throbbing immobilisation on the precipice;
chests sit with tautness born in worlds of sounds
and scents, where breath escapes without ever being captured.

Memory is always ready to spring along
the same trembling lines, but the sweat comes from motion;
the heart beats from exertion; breath quickens but
it's okay.

No one's screaming.

Alzheimer's

Angela Rose

Recognition flashed
between you and I that afternoon.
The breeze swept cool, calm, around your box room.
Your rippled fingertips: I rubbed their ridges against my palm.
The breeze swept, the bleach filled my nostrils and you were
staring.
Recognition flashed
and then it waned, sucked back down and swallowed,
but still, I felt the ridges.
Recognition flashed
it flashed, flashed, flashed, and then it burst,
grey.

Olive Skin

Harriet McInerney

When she arrives at his place the air is dense. The day is bursting
through the walls. Standing on the bathroom tiles relieves heat, a
little. In the kitchen, the light comes in through venetian blinds in
pencil lines, bisecting the smooth curves of their bodies. He holds a
hand filled with ice cubes. The ice cubes burn cold in his palms. He
rests one on each of her shoulders and she shivers and tries not to
move. As they melt she cannot tell if the water is trickling through
her t-shirt or if she can just feel her sweat. They laugh as the melted
ice trickles down her arms, her shoulders, and nibbles gently at
flushed flesh.

Walking out of the bathroom later she feels the towel nibbling
at her skin. He has green bath towels and every time she wears one
she feels like a fresh olive, bursting with flavour. Glowing under a
Grecian sun. She always takes a quiet delight in this feeling.

Later, he rolls over in bed and tells her she is like a freshly
plucked fruit, 'so vibrant'. Her smile spreads like nectar. He too
must have noticed how closely she resembles a little olive, and was
just waiting till she looked ripe to say so. She is glad he has noticed
this similarity, but he says no, he can see no olive in her. To him she
is a buoyant peach: plump and juicy. She doesn't understand and
tries to explain her olive theory again, even bringing a towel out
to hold against her skin. Little streaks of sunlight whisper across
their bodies. 'No', he says with a grin, 'you're peachy'. He continues
to smile at his own pun and she loses faith in him. She is clearly an
olive, tender and savory, small but flavoursome.

How To Fix a Watch

Harriet McInerney

Buy your watch. It costs five Euros and comes from a Dutch
street vendor. When you pay he will give you two spare batteries,
explaining how to change them. He will speak to you in Dutch, and
you won't understand, but he is lovely and somehow you depart
with his wet kiss on your cheek. The wind in Amsterdam is icy, and
when it hits your face the wetness is expansive.

In Berlin you will stay out too late, or not late enough. It is your
last night in Europe after all. At seven am you are leaving the bar.
You make an exaggerated gesture. The watch flings from your wrist,
the strap breaks. You pocket it. That day everything is slow. In the
afternoon it is raining and you are at the flea market at Mauerpark,
with no umbrella. Tarpaulins sag under the weight of water. You
buy some pink elastic string to tie your watch together. When you
show your friend she tells you it's 'practical'.

Somewhere over the Indian Ocean you wake up from shallow
sleep. You put a cardigan on and the watch is pushed up to your
elbow. The elastic holding your watch together is loose by now.
Time pushes and pulls in the stale, drowsy air.

Your watch stops soon after you get back home. You say:
whatever, five euros well spent. Maybe it worked best in European
time anyway. But your boyfriend tells you he will fix it. From then
on every time you visit it is sitting on his coffee table. The summer
is glistening, timeless. You are living off the sun's movement
through the sky. But sometimes you fall asleep at the beach. When
the sun goes down you find yourself running late.

Summer ends. You break up. You find yourself in his room
collecting your things. On top of a stack of your books is the watch.
Fixed. Time is running. Summer pollen will be on your dress, and
you won't know how it got there. But you brush it off and depart
with a wet kiss on your cheek. In Sydney the wind is warm, and
when your fingers touch your face and it feels dry and smooth.

Exit Interviews for Jobs they Don't Advertise

Peter Walsh

– Hey.

– *So.*

– Mm?

– Tell me what you're wearing.

The stenographers worked perpetually, transcribing the audio recordings into text, which would be submitted to Mario for review. He outsourced the work to an overseas firm, a firm that had since suspected him of blackmailing on an industrial scale. Sound effects were a matter of preference, and while some omitted the [SHARP EXHALE]s and [DEEP BREATH]s that punctuated these conversations, they did record in depth any individual tics or nuances that might serve to identify *beyond all doubt* a caller who – either through self- or partner-imposed guilt – disputed the phone bill they received that month. 30¢ in the first minute, $2.25 per minute after that.

At least they did. This would be the last month – the last day! – of recordings to be transcribed. Recorded for what? Posterity? Almost no phone bills to come. The truth was it wasn't profitable, not anymore. A service that had since forever littered the back pages of local newspapers and music broadsheets was dead, or dying, made obsolete by broadband and private browsing. Mario still listened in, though. The month wasn't up and there remained quotas to fill. The receiver was cradled between shoulder and ear, his hands occupied by clipboard and pen. On his desk, the phone's dock had no numbers to dial, but instead twenty flashing buttons, each button numbered and associated with a voice. A lit button indicates CALL IN PROGRESS, unlit the opposite. Flashing indicated to Mario that MARIO WAS LISTENING IN.

He pushed #13: 'You're a *dirty rotten* – '. The monitor on the desk read four minutes and from the grunts and the gradual rising of pitch he knew it'd be done by six. Tick on the page, #13 on track to meet quota. Onto #14, reaching the thirtieth minute, the disembodied voice crying on the other end and the operator cooing into the phone,

'Ohh, someone would be *lucky* to have *you*.'

The perverts, while lucrative, couldn't compare with the sad-sacks, some of whom would call once to get off before calling back again later to voice their seeded guilt. Still cheaper than a psychologist for the first forty minutes.

He rarely listened to #20. Not because #20 never missed quota, but because #20 made him uncomfortable. When he did listen in, he did so only to confirm his discomfort. Sometimes, he would listen in and hear a husky voice of experience, an older woman who conveyed an intimation of brunette with large breasts; other times he would hear the dainty fragile intonation that evoked pigtails and short shorts, jailbait or pretending to be. But #20 had a penis, was a man, and merely *put it on*. Though Mario knew this when he hired him – there was no artifice – and hired him anyway. #20 who was indispensable because he was versatile. #20 who took requests, could embody any personality within a kaleidoscope of pornographic stereotype. #20 who kept to himself mostly and didn't ask for anything.

Mario's office, a stained glass door with his name embossed, looked out upon an open plan floor space with a closed plan aesthetic. Where open plans had low-rise dividers between desks, Mario had gone for a Catholic Church confessional vibe. The walls that divided booths were soundproofed on both sides and rose from floor to ceiling, and the office space was a maze, each operator taught only the directions from the entrance to their desk, and from both to Mario's office and the bathroom. His employees enjoyed their discretion and began and finished shifts at staggered intervals. Only Mario knew just how many voices were employed.

He had no idea what would happen to the floor space, only that it had been sold. He knew the last shift would be finishing soon and they would, instead of leaving, be coming by for their exit interviews. Mario, who suffered chronic bouts of nostalgia, had never suffered more severely than now at the conclusion of what had been his working life. Mario would call them in one by one, they would sit down, he would pour them a drink – not champagne, but bubbly – and ask them to, in their own words, give him some sense of what they had heard.

* * *

#8: My name's [REDACTED] and I've worked here twelve months. In two spurts. Eight months then four. I'd be lying if I said the job wasn't taxing. The reason I quit the first time was that my partner and I, our relationship imploded over it. He knew what I was doing, I was honest, and it didn't bug him at all. He'd call sometimes, not me but the hotline, dial and re-dial till he got me. We wouldn't talk dirty or anything, he knew I found it exhausting so he'd call, pay whatever-a-minute, ask me how my day was. We'd talk for fifteen, half an hour, an hour once. It was nice. We were living together and divided the amenities – he, phone and internet; me, water and electricity – and I always felt guilty that he took the phone. So one month I made up my mind to reimburse him. Got the mail, opened the statement, and… well, when I saw how much it cost and how often he called I knew he'd spent more time talking to them than me. I had to take a break after that –

#4: – I swear my mind now lives in the gutter. Walking here, all I could think about was how I'm contributing to an *oral history* –

#1: – I see that phone every time I come by. See the lights and the numbers. Wonder which one I am. Flashflashflash. [PAUSE] Hm, 1's dead, so I guess I'm #1. Figured, I've been here – what? Years and years. And before that somewhere else. [EXHALE] All that time, I've only seen one other person. In the elevator: she was late and I early. I bet you gave her hell. She was a lot younger than I am, *was*, still is. I've aged alongside the clientele. You have too, have you noticed? Seemed we got a lot more young callers before. I used to think they made me feel old, but now it's the old ones who make me feel old. The girl I saw, the corners of her lips turned up in a smile. That was her face at rest. Looked happy even when she was pacing the elevator. Is she still here? [EXHALE] How would you know? I don't even have her name –

#13: – You wouldn't believe the calls. You wouldn't, I'm telling you. The kids who ring and try to gruff their voice into the lowest register, sometimes scores of them sniggering on the line (*shh-shh they can* hear *you*) on sleepovers or play dates, and if you imagine, you can see them sitting beneath the dining table or in the closet, the cord trailing behind them – or not trailing behind, they're cordless nowadays. You can see their parents pick up the phone and listen in. They realise what's going on, declare their presence on the line by yelling their child's name. It's enough of a surprise for the kid – poor kid – to terminate the call then and there. And these calls, the ones that die, they leave you wondering. About the kids and their parents, and whether their parents' outrage was puritan or miserly or both. Sometimes they don't hang up at all and it all plays out on conference call. You'd be foolish to hang up, just lean back and listen in. These minutes come easily – you don't have to say a word –

#8: – After a while I came back. My current partner knows what I do and doesn't approve. I think it's better that way –

#16: – He'd ring a couple times a week and ask for a young, nubile lass, and that's what I sound like so he gets me. Spits nastiness, hyperventilates over the phone. Comes, weakly… Phone drops from his hand. Line goes dead. When it's happening I don't mind it, but it creeps up on me, sticks in the back of my head. When you kiss someone deeply, tongue and all, and they've got bad breath, that awful taste lingers. At the back of your throat. When you breathe out you taste the ickiness. That's him to me… I can't hang up on a client. Or I can, but you'd want to know *why*. We've spoken about this before, you told me *not to take it personally*. It's an easy way to reach quota, so I don't. Or try not to –

#20: – I've always tried to extract myself from the calls. When I'm portraying a woman, that's just a character. And me? I'm the observer, watching the conversation play out. One time though, I couldn't help but become involved. See, this woman called up – I couldn't believe it, a woman – and she wanted to talk to a woman. What are the chances? And it piqued my interest. I thought she'd figure me out in an instant. I've always thought that I got away with putting on the voices not because I'm good at it but because the people – the men – who dial in have a vested interest in me being what I claim to be. Anything else would be shattering to their cast-iron conception of their own heterosexuality. Think about it: they dial a hotline staffed by people who they rationally know to be disinterested liars and then convince themselves that what we're saying is true. That these hot young women are really wearing what they say they are. That these women are actually women, and not like me. You say the same things, sometimes to the same callers, and they work as if they were new. That I would do *anything* to be with the caller if I could. That they should stay on the line because all the other callers are *so boring*. Imagine what they'd say if they could see me. And I'm sure they can hear tinges of it in my voice, even when I'm perky and bubbly and cute. Mostly I think it's because they're lonely, and have learned to ignore it. A peculiar form of self-preservation where they convince themselves you're sincere, expecting you to do the same, and you both exchange questions, and interests, and justify the other's presence on the line. And so your sense of self-worth becomes reiterative, like stale air circulating, the product of fans arranged in a circuit around a room. And if you're lonely and willing to pay? –

#7: – It was what it was, while it lasted –

#4: – When I first started I was so paranoid about being recognised in public. I was always on the lookout for people giving me funny looks. I've-heard-you-moan-and-talk-shit looks. I developed these anxious feelings about speaking to people I didn't know and the feelings persisted for a while. Finally, they evaporated during a trip to the bank. The teller, see, he was a caller, a regular too, and

I looked him dead in the eye as we spoke. No realisation, nothing. Either he knew and knew that any recognition would be destruction, mutually-assured, for us both; or he didn't, and would never. I haven't worried since –

#20: – And I wrongly assumed that she was immune to all this, that she'd see right through, laugh wryly, ask to be transferred to an *actual* woman and I'd laugh, drop the façade, say *no worries* mannishly and leave it at that. She didn't. Not the first time, or any time after that, even when she started calling daily. So I kept it up. We talked sexily at first and that took some getting used to, I couldn't reel off the same lines. For the first time I had to think and thinking drew me into it. After a while, we just talked about us. Or rather, she talked about her and I lied. She told me her first name, [RE-DACTED], and I made one up for me. No last names, nothing else. That we were functionally anonymous to one another allowed us to be honest – or her to be. I developed a real sense of who she was. Like, I know about the boys who came before she realised she liked girls. Or, I know that she finds movies irrepressibly boring. Things like that, peripheral things. I've never seen her, that's the truth, but I've squirreled away a stocktake of description, head-to-toe, and if I could draw I could draw something representative. I came to anticipate her calls. To be honest, my performances slipped a little – I'd hurry other callers along, terminate calls if I had to. You probably didn't notice, she and I spoke long enough to offset the dip. The problem was – and I identified it quite early – that I was falling for her, and she for an idea of me. Soon enough it happened, she wanted to meet up; and I, knowing that being a woman was a necessary condition of meeting her, knew that I couldn't possibly measure up. I'd passed the point of no return, so far as honesty was concerned. No, I'm underselling it, I'd basically crafted an image of myself – as a woman – so complex that I filled a notebook with the details of it, in dot points, under headings, so I could keep track of the lies I told. I knew I was beyond an out. You know what happened next. I came to you, told you all of it. Retired the voice and the name. Was told to move on. But I had this hope, a narcissistic one, that her feelings – hurt as I know they would've been – could have changed her nature, made her do something dramatic, have her swear off women forever, and then we'd cross paths, gender no longer a necessary condition. It was a bastard, melodramatic hope, one I'm ashamed of having had –

* * *

When the last one left, Mario paused the recorder to change tapes, withdrew the old one, labelled it and boxed it away with the others. His office was mostly bare, now. Just his table, his chairs, the cords from his phone jutting naked from the walls, walls bordered by boxes of files and tapes that would be soon deposited into his garage. A budding ecosystem of mould and silverfish waiting to emerge. He took the microphone by its stand and rotated it towards himself. Most of what he had heard he knew already, from listening in before. A lot of it he had just forgotten. #20 wasn't the first one to complain about a regular caller. When they did, he would block the number. He was aware of the revenue he conceded with every blocked call and had considered – but never implemented – an alternative. Maybe they wouldn't be shutting down had he had it in him to lie about resolving each complaint. To send the complainer back to their desk, pick up the phone and call in someone else with a similar voice, give them the back-story and a copy of the recordings to clue in to. Mario was technically capable of screening the calls as they came in. He could have put the complained-about regulars on another line with another operator, one who would pretend to be the same voice from before. It would have worked for a while, Mario imagined, before the caller realised they were being conned and develop a retrospective doubt about the whole affair, wonder if the voice they thought they were speaking to was actually two or many voices, each individually – yet communally, insidiously – conning them.

But when Mario went to recall the faces of the operators he had only just seen, he stumbled upon a similar doubt. He could no longer call directly on their individual features, nor their individual voices, but was instead left with a warbled collective voice – a reverberating, echoing voice, equal parts #1 through #20. Not just this #1 and this #20, but the #1s through #20s that existed before (Mario's number system had been present since the company's inception). Maybe he was just tired. But even #20 had receded beyond reach, was less a developed memory than an intimation of one. Mario could only partly recall his voice, and feared that concentrating upon it too hard would abstract it and render it meaningless data in his head, like when you roll a word around too long and it tastes funny in your mouth. The tapes – he still had those. And this – his recording – he still had this. He looked at the indicator on his desk; saw he had time enough left to speak and record before the fresh tape ran out and what'd been recorded would spool on in an infinite loop around the machine. Mario, with closed eyes, narrated these and other thoughts into the microphone and finally chose, however choicelessly, imagination over recollection. He visualised the faces of the faithful who must now – especially now – be trying to call in but hearing nothing but disconnection. What would seem like a momentary lapse in service would become something else with every failed call, until eventually, after days, weeks, months, they would realise it was over. So they'd hang up, and say half-heartedly that they were through, and then mostly wouldn't dial in anymore dial in anymore dial in anymore dial in anymore –

Any Other Day

Rebecca Georgiades

> 'He who is of a calm and happy nature will hardly feel the
> pressure of age, but to him who is of an opposite disposition,
> youth and age are equally a burden.' –Plato

'It's over now.'

The air is clinical. Emotionless. And I can't help feeling that oxygen is being drawn from my lungs. You'd think I'd be used to it by now. Hours of mental exhaustion never cease to leave a heavy footprint behind.

The machines' humming comes to a pause before the next row of youths take their seats. Their heads hang heavily, their bodies stiff. Yet the only sign of their exhaustion is the dark shadows which envelop their eyes, the colour of bruised plums recovered from the bottom of a bag. They're almost transparent, ghost-like, and I wonder whether I'm gazing at my reflection. It's been years since all mirrors and reflective instruments were destroyed. They say that these were the first reforms implemented after The Ascension. They say that they wither at their reflections.

By the time we are escorted out from the Labour Headquarters, a thick darkness blankets the city, suffocating any visible form of life that hasn't yet retreated. The descriptions of nightlife within the city in the Anarchy Days are frowned upon. They say the youths plagued the streets until dawn, unlike the rest of the aging population who sought comfort in their beds. The ground would shake to a rhythm of absurdly loud sounds. They say the youths brought chaos in their intoxicated states, hanging from balconies or occupying gutters. The pungent smell of urine and beer stung the nostrils of any decent passers-by. The city was transformed into a concrete zoo; the main attraction, a meandering bare-footed animal with any sense of civility lost within their vacant gaze. The monthly

Gratitude Festival consisted of broadcasting a short documentary, which reminded us of the vulgar and immoral behaviour of youths during the Anarchy Days. A tradition for as long as I remember. Eight Days. It would all be happening again.

As I await the bus to our living quarters, I shudder as my memories of the last broadcast become real and creep like a vine, meandering, twisting in my mind. Those voices, resonating off the building walls, reminding me of the filth I supposedly created. The broadcast ends with the image of an elderly man with grey curled hair, beating his gavel on a wooden bench as he sentences the delinquents to overflowing prisons, rather lenient for their disgusting crimes, so we're told. The sound of the gavel engulfs the city square, echoing within the hearts of each of the youths, who simultaneously shuddered in repulse. The shame thickens within their throats.

As I board the bus, I consider my favourite part of the festival: the parade following the broadcasting. The youths are marched along the remains of George Street, named after the good King George III, the ancient sovereign of our land almost 800 years ago. As we march, the street is transformed into a river of orange uniforms. Thousands of Elders line the streets, praising us for our daily labour. Those that can stand leaning into the railings, smiling through thin lips. When the road ends, the city comes to a standstill; even the royal flags obey the silence. This is when our breath stops as the Elder Monarchs emerge through the Palace's doorway, built on the ancient site of what was known as the Queen Victoria Building, destroyed in the Anarchy fires of the youth rebellion. All that remains is the antique clock, decorated with a four-turret stone castle, suspended from the roof in a glass cabinet. The clock chimes each hour, pulsating through the city's veins, motivating each youth to labour more vigorously to prevent the doomed fate of the Elders.

I remember my discomfort at the last parade as I craned my neck upwards, the sun blurring my vision as I tried to catch a glimpse of the monarchs. It didn't matter that our heads ached, we revelled in the loud projection of the King's voice. Like those of the Elder elite, his voice was aged and wise as he proclaimed the words which were first declared by the Elders after The Ascension.

'We gather here today under the united flag of Aeternam to raise the memory of the foul and heinous deeds the youth committed, and to most fervently remind each of you that free thinking is a most horrible thing, which will transform you into dangerous creatures. On this note, on behalf of the Elders, I humbly thank you for the cooperation you deliver daily, and of course for the contribution of you who labour towards our longevity.'

He then proceeded to reward the youth that devised the most innovative plan to reverse the Elders' aging clock. The most meritorious innovation occurred a decade ago. Glial Reconstitution. A monthly infusion into the circulating cerebrospinal fluid of each Elder, tripling the amount of glial cells so that each neuron remained insulated, protected and supplied with triple the nutrients. In short, the minds of each of the elders Elder were as active and young as they were in their earlier adult life.

'One at a time. Get on with it now.'

I'm jolted into the present by the sound of his voice as we queue in search of space on the bus. He furrows his sparse eyebrows, his forehead becoming a lined memoir of the expressions of his life; each thin crease a memory he gained over the decades. If I persist, searching into his pale eyes, I almost see into the vacant room of his youthful soul.

'Eyes to the ground!' He indicates with his staff, showering the air with spittle.

As we all shuffle into the remaining pockets of space, we begin the long silent commute to our living quarters. Within the windows' reflection I notice a girl's faltering figure struggling to balance. She reminds me of myself when I had been introduced into this life of intellectual serfdom forcing daily innovation. In another forty-two years I'll reach Elderdom, where I'll receive respect, wealth, and be granted the rite of open thinking. All of which I'd treat irresponsibly if received now.

The drone of the bus lulls me and my eyes feel heavy, but nothing can remove the constant pounding in my head. Aches in this region are common in our lives now. The pain feels rewarding, reminding me of the sacrifice I give up daily in my labour.

As the half hour passes, I am awoken from my sleepy consciousness by two resplendent lights burning into my eyes. Then contact. It all happens in less than a second, and suddenly the bus is soaring over the bridge. Time uncannily slows and all I can focus on is a footless orange shoe, suspended, twirling through the air, to the sound of moans and screaming. The water engulfs us, stubbornly pushing its way through the open windows. The shoe bounces on top of the water. Climbing. Climbing. Until it floats up to my hips. I realise I have no idea how to stay afloat. I scramble my way to balance on the back of the metal seats, and notice I'm not the only one who has realised this and taken my thoughts to their terrifying conclusion. I look for a solution in the bus driver's face. He is almost the age of Elderdom, at which he'd give up this lifestyle. I see him sitting motionless in his seat and realise he has given up not just his lifestyle but his life.

'We…we need to wait until it's full of water.'

The words flee from my throat, bent towards the roof. I'm shocked I still had a voice after not using it for so long.

After it's filled with water we can escape through the windows!' I'm now shouting. Something so forbidden, I would've lost a hand if it were any other day.

I realise I have no audience. The water engulfs me, its icy chill biting my skin. The lights flicker. Darkness.

* * *

Again fluorescent lights awaken me from my unconsciousness. Bright and unfriendly through my eyelids. The first thing I sense is the unfamiliar dressings wrapped around my forehead. Although my head aches from the blow I apparently received, my thoughts have developed a new sense of clarity. Everything seems so much louder. Sharper.

'We can't let her go on like this. She needs to labour at the soonest possible time. It's been days ... you very well know what thoughts she'll begin developing.'

The whisper is fast and forcefully hostile.

'But she's in no position to work, it could do irreversible –'

'I make the rules. When I return I want to see her wired up.'

'Yes.'

That was it. Three letters which had such control over my immediate future.

As the footsteps faded in the distance, I knew it was safe to open my eyes.

'Good. You are awake.'

I immediately regret my decision. She approaches from the corner, a fresh Elder, probably just entered her sixty-first year.

'Your name is ISA-137, of region thirteen, block seven and you have been in a minor accident. Nonetheless, I assume you're eager to return to your labour. Your daily contribution has been missed,' she explains. Her eyes cannot disguise her lies or contempt which bores itself into my soul.

As she attaches the probes to my bald scalp I envisage the short curls that frame her face on my scalp instead. The loss of our hair is of course for practical reasons, so that the wires can be attached more effectively, but still I long for the day when I receive this rite. Envy? Impossible, I'm incapable of Elder emotions. I shake the thought away.

She places the intellectual drawing-screen on my lap then exits the room. The heavy burden of devising longevity treatments weighs down heavily upon my shoulders. It's too heavy today and at once I move the screen aside. I notice the lack of the machine's constant humming, usually produced when its operating system is on. In a moment of sheer forgetfulness on her behalf, it seems to be a complete moment of luck; no headaches for me today.

I count down the hours as the hands march around the clock. I imagine the small cogs rotating in different directions within. I'm overcome with an unfamiliar feeling of complete disinterest.

Boredom, the Elders term it. The Elder's footsteps approach from down the hallway and in the remaining seconds I sketch a complex diagram accompanied with chemical equations: the last project I remember working on, however many days ago.

She re-enters the room, clearly unaware she forgot to turn the machine on, and proceeds to remove the probes that should have mapped my brain activity. Up close, through her sparse curls, I notice the small tattoo of the royal crest; the King's silhouette imprinted on the Fountain of Youth, branded into the back of her scalp. GWN-139. She once came from the same labour region as me. I suddenly feel somewhat connected. I wonder why I've never previously seen her? Instantly I feel the sting of her slap burning hot on my cheek. Her eyes fixated on mine.

I react like I would any other day, too exhausted, yet managing to thank her for disciplining a prying youth.

Her eyes draw towards my cheek that I imagine to be red hot against the surrounding paler skin. She speaks again. Her voice is an instrument of measure and control.

'That's not who I am anymore. GWN-139,' she recites, 'was a pathetic and dangerous creature as you are now. But within you is a more controlled human, released once you have done your duty to the realm.'

A figure bursts into the room. 'ISA-137?'

He walks confidently to the side of my bed and I recognise his voice as the earlier hostile tone. I manage a nod.

'Elder Dr Garwin,' he announces, his eyes sharp against wiry eyebrows that paint on him a permanent expression of being deep in thought. Constantly calculating.

'At the upcoming Gratitude Festival, which will take place in a day's time, you will be awarded with the most innovative anti-aging treatment … quite a breakthrough. It's already been implemented and showed very effective promising results.'

He manoeuvres his white coat and shirt to the side, revealing the outline of the small magnetic box I'd devised, which has already been installed inside his chest. The surrounding areas of grey hair are freshly shaven.

I react like I would any other day. Speechless. My eyes cast down, focusing on his polished shoes, concealing the excitement and pride bubbling in my throat. The strangest and most extraordinary feeling. So this is what prides feels like? My project was aimed at exploring what specific hindrance, within a human, signalled a body to begin its perpetual journey to decay. What signalled one's skin to take up the appearance of a crinkled paper bag? What signalled one's hair to become a scattered thin silver forest? But most importantly, what signalled the switching off of one's vital organs?

All these questions led me to the discovery of Horology Kinase, an enzyme whose sole purpose is to signal the human body's slowing down. The life clock. With the instalment of a small magnetic box I created, a human's HK enzymes froze in time. No signal to ever ring the doorbell of Death. It was the immortal drink from the Fountain of Youth. Eternal life.

'You must now exit the premises and of course remain ever grateful for the services that you have received. Board a bus immediately and return to your region.' He disappears from my sight.

I peel back the sheet. The tiles are icy beneath my feet. I dress in the familiar orange. As I walk through the exit doors, the two Elder guards shove me onto the gutter. One of them coughs up spittle that puddles itself at my feet. A foreign urge to attack and defend myself works itself into my now clenched fists. I quickly dismiss it. Reacting like I would any other day, I recoil and hastily walk towards the bus.

Once seated, my hands become a moist canvas. My forehead throbs and a trickle of blood beads up along the sliced scar. The fear drips down my neck and I find myself getting off the bus at the earliest stop.

I try to blend in with the other youths shuffling, head down, in a scrambled mess towards their living quarters. The streets and buildings of Region 1 are eerily clean. The sound of the overhead monorail whirrs its way along the track. My attention is drawn to the distinguished sound of the brake pads and suspension coils as they shrink bouncing back as an automobile turns a corner a few streets ahead. Then suddenly I imagine the blueprints of a nearby elevator's cables, each steel thread intertwined connecting to the counter weight. My mind ticks, calculating the forces. It's no doubt that our brains have reached an intellectual pinnacle.

A nearby menacing laugh disturbs my thoughts. I turn and see that its owner is a crooked Elder jeering at the youth prisoners in Region 1's public square. Their translucent thin little arms and necks hang in the iron stocks. Above each of them, glowing in the darkness, are LED labels. 'Lazy.' 'Plagiariser.' 'Procrastinator.' Whilst ridiculing the youths, the Elder manages to pick up stones amongst the gravel, throwing them at the youths' faces causing blood to seep from their cuts.

Before I notice, the ground and buildings around me are blurry. I'm running, with any sense of destination lost within the unfamiliar moisture seeping down my cheeks. At the turn of a corner I find myself surrounded by the dark nothingness extending as far as my eyes can see. I stand in the middle of Aeternam's restricted Wasteland. A few scattered ruins draped with rubbish and biohazardous chemicals. I trip and stub my toe on an object set rolling into a small scrap of moonlight. A skull. A small skull, a young skull, shining ivory in the fractured light. My eyes adjust and I realise another ten, twenty, thirty skulls surround me. A graveyard of rusted metal, history and the stolen dreams of the exploited youth. The smell overwhelms me and a guttural and harrowing scream boils from my mouth, its lumps tasting bitter upon my tongue. I know I've seen something I wasn't supposed to. But maybe I was? I know what has to be done.

* * *

My ID number is projected clearly through the speakers, bouncing off the surrounding high rise buildings. I crane my neck upwards like I would any other day. I ascend the palace stairs to shake the King's hand. One by one until he stands so close that the pungent smell of his cologne tingles my nostrils. I reach into my pocket and rub my thumb over and over, circling the detonator. Every headache, slap, and spittle that landed on my shoes culminates into a vigorous surge of pressure as I press down the button.

The detonator triggers a pulse of magnetic radiation frying each magnetic box within the Elders and forcing the Horology Kinase within them to work in overdrive. Each is activated, and accelerated hundreds of years into the future. Like the hands of a clock sprinting to the finish line. Death.

In a split second the King's eyes turn dull. His calloused skin begins to crumble in small flakes, floating in the light breeze. From his crusting mouth roars one last tortured cry of rotting breath until larger shreds of skin break loose from his now gaunt face, and the whole surface of his body falls into pieces creating a pile of dirty brown ash. His bones collapse to the ground, turning greyer and greyer until they too are camouflaged in the pile of dust. Only his jewels remain, coated in a thin sheen of ashes.

Around me the dust of the street begins to settle itself in large piles where the Elders stood.

I wipe the dust from my upper lip. Today is not any other day.

Rib

Hal Conyngham

You
in the whale
in the earth under earth
screaming and scratching and calling and clawing
with splinters under your fingernails
and flakes of dried, peeling paint falling onto your forehead and
cheekbones
choking in your nostrils

the sun was borne earth though it lives in sky
think seed think idea think child
think clay that is earth
think clay that was earth
surrogate blue, surrogate sky
unprophet unparent
I am not your child
I am not noble
I was not made of stars

your hair is birds-nest knitted spiders web
your fingers frostbite-broken, nails whispered shells
chrysalis closes every once in a while
then puppet-jerks, sprung
as you almost fall
you can't feel your feet.

infant/infant/newborn/infant/infant/baby/embryo/newborn/
baby
but to say – child
but to say – child, you are not yourself
    breaks me

child, you are not
            newborn
    – child, you are ancient
  you live through bones of giants
  you speak through respun lips
your leg is not yours
your cheek is not yours
your spine is not yours
but hair that was fingers that were ribs
        – child, god is Frankenstein
        and you are held by stitching

  the whale in you
as she spouts, you drown.

Enduring

Maddie Houlbrook-Walk

It is harder than you'd think to
float atop the Salt Sea.
I always paddle with clenched fists;
I keep my spirit in my hands because
there's no room in my head.
I wade with breezeblocks
in my chest, when this ocean feels like sand
against my skin.

I sense distant tremors and shift.
Why stand my ground when
I can rocket from the
ocean to the sun?
Sharing my excitement with
whales in slow motion,
I keep my fists clenched
to save this energy that torrents
from my fingertips.

I am always
watching the waves that
pound my walls.
The moon swings tides to
wash over me until
I feel salt in my bones.
I look right at the sun to keep afloat.

I am often alone out at sea.

My lungs must be empty
before I can drown.

The Human Festival

Drew Rooke

Atop Allahabad's Shashtri Bridge, crossing the Ganga River,
I first see the world's largest gathering of humans. Taupe and
multicoloured tarpaulin-shielded tent camps sprawl below,
reaching the railway bridge 200 metres away and disappear into
Allahabad's carpeting morning mist. They fill every visible space
and I can just make out the muddy road and the traffic of people,
which run through these canvas houses as the bus speeds along.

This is the Maha Kumbh. A Kumbh occurs once every three
years at four alternate locations across India: Nasik, Ujjain,
Haridwar and Allahabad. Every twelve years is a *purna* (full)
Kumbh held only at Allahabad, and a Maha Kumbh happens
only after twelve purna Kumbh's, every 144 years. The 2013
Maha Kumbh, then, is the most significant event in the lifetime
of millions of Hindus across India and the world. No wonder I
struggled to prepare myself. I knew the festival would be enormous
in both size and spirit, but I quickly realised I had grossly
underestimated it.

The sight from the bridge was just one sector of Maha Kumbh.
One of fourteen sectors. The festival covers 1937 hectares, has
56.2km of temporary road and for the forty-four days it is to run,
100 million pilgrims are expected to attend. Thirty of these million
come for *Mauni Amawasya*, the main bathing day, held on the 10th
of February.

Thirty million people at a festival on *one day,* all here to bathe
at the Triveni Sangam, the confluence of India's holiest rivers:
the Ganga, the Yamuna and the mythical Saraswati. To cleanse
their sins. To purify themselves. To embody god. To reach *moksha* (liberation). Thirty million people. Seven million more than
Australia's total population. An incomprehensible figure.

Such a mass of people drowns the tiredness and exhaustion I
feel after waking up at four a.m. to witness the bathing of the Naga

Sadhus on the banks of the Sangam. The Naga Sadhus are the most devout Hindus who wear nothing but ash and are known as the 'Protectors of the Faith'. I exit my ashram onto the road outside and the overpowering current of human traffic going south seizes me. One way only. I surrender my freedom of movement to Kumbh Mela. It takes control of my feet, of my entire body.

Personal space is extinguished as sweaty skin rubs perpetually against mine. Patterned flags and tree branches are held up by the leader of a family or a group, the only identification in this sea of anonymity. The unified scuff of thirty million feet rises with the dust hovering in the air, penetrating the scarf I have wrapped around my head and filling my throat. I start coughing, phlegm rising from my lungs, but there is nowhere to spit. Feet, legs, bodies everywhere. Above the deafening mantras being chanted, I can hear shouts for lost children and loudspeakers blaring directions to the Sangam. Kumbh Mela tells me to swallow. I oblige.

Streetlights flicker overhead, the air a pious glowing orange. Beside me, a father and mother balance their bags on their heads, their two sons frightened, cling to their parents' tender, comforting hands. They walk as one.

The shouting ahead mutes the family's whispered mantras. I raise my head above the crowd and see chaos building at an approaching major intersection. A pileup of human traffic. Mounted police, swamped by desperate pilgrims, frantically block the road we are on and struggle against their beasts' wishes to escape.

Forward movement slows as a push crushes from behind. Mothers hold their children tighter as we are all squeezed harder by the clenching muscle of this human current. It pushes me forward and drags me across. Families, desperate to stay together and reach the river of liberation, fight to get through. It is an all-ages wrestling match on the grandest scale: men, women and children jostling, shoving and screaming. The intersecting traffic takes hold of me and I scramble to push out. But it is in vain. Being alone I am lucky, and surrender to this new rip, riding it slowly to the Sangam.

The river quells the chaos. Just the sight of it massages us. It breathes tranquility, serenity and calmness so suddenly that I forget the chaotic anarchy. Choking dust is replaced by soft sand, motherly screams by meditative mantras, and pungent sweat by sandalwood incense and *charas*. Bright orange marigold petals wash through the legs of the bathers who are silhouetted in the morning dawn, immune to the chilly air of Indian winters.

It is an almighty scene and brews within me an irresistible urge to join. Stripping down to my underwear, I walk into the icy water. Waist deep, eyes closed, the water caresses and energises. I dip my head under the water three times, one for each family member, as told to do by a fellow bather. The rising sun warms my skin and the thousands of those around me.

I turn to the kaleidoscopic riverbank. Baby blue, turquoise, violet, lemon yellow and rose red saris dry in the wind. Pilgrims stand tall, their bodies golden from the rays of the rising sun. Splashed droplets from the river form crystals in the air. The morning sky behind the bank is a soft indigo, and I walk the line of the reflecting sunrise back to the bank.

Drying myself, a smiling, elderly Brahmin man wearing an orange *longyi* approaches. 'How do you feel?' he asks.

I answer immediately and effortlessly. 'Refreshed and rejuvenated.'

'That is Kumbh,' he replies, wobbling his head and walking off.

* * *

What is Kumbh? I ponder this for the next five days at the festival. I stop at a chai walla as I am walking to the Ganga on my final morning and meet Robin Swami. He is a twenty-one-year-old accounting student, well-spoken in English, from Jaipur who travelled to Kumbh Mela in a group of seventy. Squatting next to me and cupping a chai, his eyes widen, cheeks dimple and white teeth shine as a smile beams from his face. I ask what the *Samudra Manthan* (the episode behind Kumbh) involves.

'The *devas* [gods] and *asuras* [demons] were fighting over *amrita* [the nectar of immortality] from the *Kshira Sagar* [Ocean of Milk],' Robin says joyously as the chai walla brings me a cup of sweet, spicy tea.

'The fight went for twelve days and nights which is the same as twelve human years. Four drops of *amrita* fell at the places where the Kumbh's are now held.'

I ask if Kumbh is just this for him or if it is more.

'When I bathe at the Sangam, I meet my god. I see him. I get life flowing through me. I feel very lucky to make it here,' he replies.

I point to the plastic bottle full of murky water he has between his legs. 'What is that for?'

'This is the water of the Sangam for my family back home. Many couldn't make it, so I am taking this back for them. Inside is our god.'

I left Robin with some answers to my question, but nothing definite. I knew religion was fundamental to Kumbh and it was what drew pilgrims here. But even as a non-believer, I still shared their invigoration and excitement from being there. What exactly is Kumbh, then?

I meet Triveni Shashikant outside my ashram on my final morning. He is the owner of a handicrafts store in Varanasi and a devout Hindu. This was his third Kumbh Mela. I put my question to him.

'It is more a human festival than just a Hindu or religious one. When you are at Kumbh Mela, you feel the human system of love and compassion working. People go to find moksha, and many do. But at the same time, they discover what the human sentiment of being together, being connected, is all about.'

A wailing mother enters the ashram as we speak. Triveni, deciphering her cries, tells me she has lost her three children on the walk to the festival from Allahabad train station and has no place to stay. I watch as *Babaji* (the head guru of the ashram) sits her down and consoles her. Triveni inquires and reveals to me that Babaji will help her find her children and has invited them to stay at the ashram free of charge – like every ashram around the festival.

'Case in point,' Triveni laughs.

And he is right. Kumbh is about the human sentiment, the human spirit. Compassion, altruism and community, above religion and the chaos, define it. You see it in the son carrying his disabled mother on the back of his bicycle to the Sangam, and in the paramilitary officer helping an exhausted elderly man across the road and getting him a chai. You feel it walking around the festival, sleeping harmoniously with twenty others in a crowded tent, eating lunch on lines of straw mats with hundreds of people, and bathing with millions. Everything is done communally. Life is shared. Love is shared. Electricity powers the festival's lights, but human energy powers the festival.

Barriers of wealth, caste, language and colour crumble under the pounding, loving heart of Maha Kumbh. For forty-four days, humanity and equality triumph. I do not have a new-found faith after attending the largest religious festival on earth. I remain unconverted. But I am energised by the contagious power of the human sentiment. It is that which is Kumbh.

Ellie

Micaela Brookman

Medium
Photography (digital Canon T-3I), Photoshop CS6, silk

Blurb
Ellie is a digital manipulation that teeters on the line between surrealism and reality. The central figure's porcelain skin provides a stark contrast with the vibrant orange draping and crisp blue sky that surrounds her.

Isa

Micaela Brookman

Medium
Photography (Canon AE-1), double exposure on black and white film, tungsten lighting, paper

Blurb
Isa is a hand-developed piece created using the double-exposure technique on film. This studio portrait is partially obscured by the overlaying concentric circles that dominate the image.

Untitled (36 Tetrahedra)

Sara Morawetz

Medium
Paper

Blurb
Untitled (36 Tetrahedra) is a hand-made sculpture from
computer modelling with scientist, and University of Sydney
PhD candidate Darren Engwirda. The random data sets and
computational algorithms seek to explore the incremental nature
of geometric forms and the relationship between art and science.
The development of scientific method and the philosophy upon
which it is built can be seen to contextualise the idea of art as an
experiment and as a reaction to science's fundamental principles.

Lottery series

Sara Morawetz

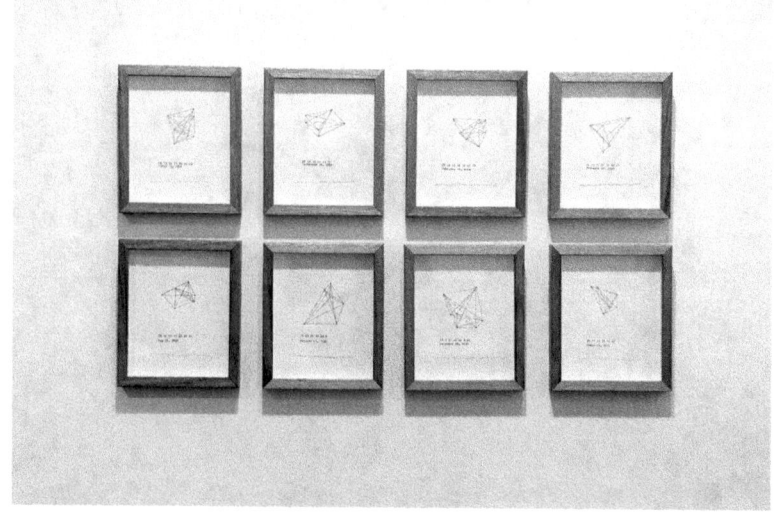

Medium

Archival pen on paper

Blurb

Lottery is an ongoing series of drawings that visualise lottery numbers in history from socially, culturally, economically or naturally significant events. The data and human algorithm generates a set of geometric visuals that construct an illusion of order, illustrating both the elements of chance and disorder in pivotal events, as well as the oblivious continuation of everyday actions.

Individual works in this series include: *April 15, 2010 (Volcanic Ash Cloud Covers Europe); December 18 2010 (Governmental Protests Begin in Tunisia, Starting What Will Later be Known as The Arab*

Spring); February 13, 2008 (Prime Minister Kevin Rudd Apologises to Aboriginal and Torres Strait Islander Australians); February 2, 2004 (Facebook Launched); January 1, 1999 (The Euro Currency is Introduced); March 11, 2011 (Undersea Megathrust Earthquake off the Coast of Japan); May 5, 2000 (Conjunction of Sun, Mercury, Venus, Mars, Jupiter, Saturn and Moon); September 16, 2001 ('This Crusade – This War on Terrorism – is Going to Take a While ... ' GW Bush).

Kazaridaru

Alexandra Banks

Medium
Photography (Olympus EPL-1)

Blurb
In Japan, sake is associated with bringing the people together with
the gods. At traditional Shinto festivals, revellers would be provided
a cup of sake to lighten the mood and make them feel closer to the
gods. Sake brewers from around Japan donate these decorative sake
barrels to commemorate the shrine's namesakes, Emperor Meiji
and Empress Shoken. This photograph features the *kazaridaru*
barrels that line the pathway to Tokyo's Meiji Jingu Shrine during
an unusually large January snowfall.

Takeshita-dori

Alexandra Banks

Medium
Photography (Olympus EPL-1)

Blurb
Tokyo's Takeshita Street, located in the centre of Harajuku, is the centre of Japan's youth culture. Despite over fifteen centimetres of snow having fallen on a bitter January morning grinding traffic and trains to a halt, this popular shopping boulevard was packed with teenagers and tourists huddling under clear plastic umbrellas.

Man Playing Erhu

Shuhan Li

Medium

Photography (Nikon D90)

Blurb

This photo was taken in Langzhong, Sichuan province, China. Dressed in the old-fashioned way, this man kept on playing *erhu* disregarding of the crowds of tourists flashing at him. He seems to be indulged in his own world of memories of times past.

Unravel series

Kat Beaton

Medium
Acid etchings on recycled paper

Blurb
In Kat Beaton's series *Unravel*, a rabbit slowly turns into thread and entangles itself within it. Having previously explored issues of trauma and anxiety through highly confronting images, these childlike etchings express a soft timidity that touches upon living with trauma, which even the fragile nature of the recycled paper enhances. The thread is a part of the rabbit just as trauma is a part of oneself, where one is tangled up with something that can often be restrictive. Beaton wanted to create an image through which both children and adults could relate to the feeling of being entangled within one's own self.

Sapa Hills

William Hade

Medium

Photography (Sony Cybershot DSC-W80)

Blurb

Sapa Hills was taken whilst on a trip to a small town in the northern region of Vietnam. Known for its mountainous landscapes and terraced rice fields, Sapa is home to the Hmong tribe, whose style of dwelling is the focus of this work. *Sapa Hills*, charting the simplicity of rural life for the Hmongs, expounds the visceral relationship between a people and their milieu.

Mengenang

Ezreena Yahya

Medium
Photography (Canon 550D)

Blurb
Taken at last year's Sculpture by the Sea along the eastern beaches of Sydney, *Mengenang* (or 'to reflect' in Indonesian), with its tall bamboo stakes and hypnotising drumming of bird-scarers, was a standout. The girl in the photograph was a passerby, whose soft, wispy hair and comely nature caught my eye from a distance.

A Splash of Rain

Theodora Yip

Medium
Photography (Nikon D60)

Blurb
'The only noise now was the rain, pattering softly with the magnificent indifference of nature for the tangled passions of humans.' (Sherwood Smith)

Shine a Light

Katherine Johns

Medium

Photography (Nikon D60 + AF-S DX Nikkor 18–55mm Lens, no flash)

Blurb

The image was composed as part of an exercise focusing on experimentation with depth of field. Captured at night on a suburban driveway, the shot was lit using a standard flash light and captured with a Nikon D60. A Nikkor 18–55mm lens was used to create the bokeh effect in the foreground, and to capture the natural details present in the surface of the curled leaf.

Landscape of Farmers
and
Pink Girl on Shore

Aletheia Casey and Enrico Gaoni

Medium

Photography (medium-format camera, positive film)

Blurb

Iranians flock to the water during the annual Persian New Year celebrations. Many go to the Caspian Sea and others in the Northern Regions go to Lake Urmia, a body of water which is the largest salt lake in the Middle East. The massive lake lies far away from the country's capital Tehran, in the province of West Azerbaijan. The lake used to be an important feeding ground for large numbers of wildlife and birds.

Today, due to drought, irrigation and damming projects which block the water flow, Lake Urmia is emptying fast. Now the water is so far away from the shore that it takes almost half an hour to reach it by foot. The salt crunches and breaks underfoot, while the boats sit awkwardly on the salty surface of the lake, a mockery of their old lives. It is feared that if the lake dries completely the many towns and cities positioned close to the massive lake will be covered with life-threatening salt and dust which will blow straight from the lake and cover the life which once thrived.

It has recently been suggested by environmental experts that in order to save Lake Urmia from drying completely, water should be pumped all the way from the Caspian Sea to the Lake. It seems to many that this may be the only chance of saving Lake Urmia from drying totally and becoming a massive ecological disaster.

The Overlapping Lovers

Bec Eames

In the small town of Willoughby-on-Wye there is a person who is currently known by the name of Remi. Remi is thirty-five years old, has unusually thick eyebrows, wide ankles, dark secrets, and a fondness for cirrocumulus clouds. She owns a house with thatch on the roof and a pond in the back garden. There are four ducks, called Monster, Fiend, Blot, and Bertha, as well as several ducks that do not actually belong to Remi but seem to wander in and out of the garden at will. There is also Aggie, who is not a duck. Aggie has a sharp wit, a kind soul, an ailing mother, a patchy memory, and she is nocturnal. Remi is of the day and Aggie is of the night, and this would not be a problem at all except for the very inconvenient fact that they are in love.

It is a Tuesday morning, and the house is quiet. The clock on the wall is broken, but the time is five fifty-nine a.m. There is a feeling in the air as if the universe is waiting for something. Perhaps it is waiting for global warming to be quenched in the rising flames of the human conscience, or for world peace to sail into existence hailed by glorious trumpets and rains of joy and goodwill, or for Remi's snores to gutter out in the dusky haze that precedes the dawn. If this is the case then the universe is out of luck – Remi's snoring is a habit woven into the fabric of the planet, an inexorable force.

The front door bangs open.

Suddenly the house is not quiet at all. Joining the distant cacophony of Remi's snores, the clock on the wall spontaneously comes to life, ticking merrily away; the ducks in the garden begin to flap and quack; a car zooms past, beeping loudly for no apparent reason, and Aggie stumbles into the front hall, dropping her keys on the counter, kicking her shoes off into the kitchen, slumping into a chair with a clatter and a sigh. Her eyes are heavy. Her skin is slick with sweat and the traces of remembered fluids. She rubs a hand across her face, and breathes in, and checks her watch. It is seven past six. Her mouth tightens.

In a flurry of sudden movement Aggie lunges from the chair, rummaging through her bag to produce a second bag, plastic, containing a set of stained white scrubs, which she promptly throws into the washing machine, shortly followed by a cup of bleach. From the washing machine she moves to the fridge, which is opened, inspected, and, its contents judged unworthy, abandoned. Aggie resorts to a cupboard, from which she removes a box of stale cereal. She pours the cereal into a bowl and eats it dry, checking her watch between bites. It is six eleven. Six twelve. Aggie curses under her breath, tips the remaining cereal into the bin, and stalks upstairs, stripping as she goes, past an open door from which Remi's snores tumble out as if to greet her, and into the bathroom. She flicks a switch, checks her watch, and plunges into the shower, scalding water pouring across her freckled skin, into her eyes, into her mouth. Through the steam she checks her watch. The time is six fourteen.

Swiping a towel over her goose-prickling body, she emerges from the bathroom, hair dripping on the floorboards, leaving pools of water to spread into the grain of the wood. The time is six fifteen. Aggie drops her towel on the floor, and walks into the bedroom, where Remi snores on, undisturbed, the blankets rucked up around her armpits. Aggie pauses to drink in the sight of her. In the dark she is very handsome. On the bedside table there is a notepad; Aggie fishes a pen out of some crevice and scribbles a note, pressing a kiss to the page. As she does so a stray hair is dislodged from behind her ear, falling onto the paper, leaving a wet line that blurs her words. Aggie falls into the bed and studies the ceiling, which is shaking slightly with the vibration of her lover's snores. She turns her head, and studies the curve of Remi's ear, the brush of her eyelashes over dark cheeks, and checks her watch. The time is six twenty-two. Outside the window there is a renewed clamour of awakening birds, ducks and sparrows and magpies, starlings and squawking crows. The sky lightens. In the distance there is a thin smear of bright orange, rising over the hills.

Aggie shuts her eyes.

Remi's eyes open.

There is a faint stripe of sunlight spilling over the bed. Beside her, Aggie shifts and then settles. Remi lies there for a moment, breathing steadily. After a while she huffs and gets out of bed, tucking the blankets carefully back into place. She pulls the curtains shut, and the stripe of sunlight winks out as if it were never there. On the bedside table there is a notepad. The message written on it is barely legible, but Remi has had years of practice to decipher such messages. It reads:

> Out of milk. Couple of difficult patients today. Laura made
> some smarmy comments, I ignored her. Thought of you.
> Thought about the eclipse last summer. Had an idea for that
> character you were struggling with, I'll write about it when I'm
> not dead on my feet. Love, adoration, etc.

Outside, the ducks are quacking and hollering. Remi hurries downstairs, pausing at the door to slide into her slightly damp gumboots, wincing at the squish. The ducks don't shut up once they've been fed; through long experience she has learnt not to expect them to. She hunts around for a minute or two, hoping to find Bertha's stash of hidden eggs, but the search proves fruitless. Remi wonders for a moment if she should feel miffed at having been outwitted by a duck, but eventually decides that she's too sleepy to mind; besides, it's not exactly an infrequent occurrence.

After a swift and futile trawl through the kitchen, she fetches her coat and wanders out in the vague direction of the corner store, reciting a garbled mantra under her breath. The mantra goes something like this: milk eggs bread pasta cereal milk eggs pasta bread cereal eggs bread milk eggs milk. Her breath steams out in the morning air, and she spends an entertaining few minutes pretending to be a ravening dragon, roaring and stomping, before one of the ducks squawks at her in something suspiciously resembling laughter. Milk eggs bread. Remi concentrates.

By seven o'clock she is back in the kitchen, sorting the groceries into neat little piles, at which point she realises that she has forgotten to buy milk. She pauses for a moment, contemplating this. Her breakfast consists of a carefully applied scrape of marmalade across a carefully sliced piece of newly-baked bread. She eats it and contemplates some more.

After cleaning the kitchen Remi retires to her writing space. It used to be a particularly large cupboard, but they managed to fit in a computer and a window, and now it's just a particularly cramped study. For Remi it's perfect. The sun pours in at exactly the right angle, and she can hardly hear the ducks at all.

She spends a slightly frustrating morning staring at a blank computer screen and wondering about Aggie's idea. No doubt the idea is a perfect one, and the thought of its perfection taunts her. Eventually she manages to write a rather unsatisfying paragraph that she will probably have to delete later, shuts down the computer, and makes lunch. Lunch is pasta. She returns to the study. Pasta-fueled she has slightly more luck; she hashes out a scene that has been bothering her for weeks and creates an elegant plot twist. She is so proud of the plot twist that she resolves to take the rest of the day off. She spends her day off lounging on the sofa and watching an old documentary about cabbage farming. It is a very informative documentary, and after it is finished Remi feels that she knows all there is to know about cabbage. Partway through it she has a spectacular idea for a story, and snatches up the nearest piece of paper to hand, scrawling it down before she forgets the details.

All too soon the sunlight wanes, and Remi finds that she is more tired than she has ever been. She rubs a hand across her mouth. When she removes it there is a streak of drool across the knuckle of her thumb, like the lingering secretions of a snail. She checks her watch. The time is seven twenty in the evening.

Remi yawns, jaw popping, and then chokes from inhaling too much air. She goes to their bedroom and changes into worn flannel pyjamas. Aggie does not stir. The time is seven twenty-four. She lies down on the bed. She stands up again, and fetches the writing-pad from the bedside table, and scribbles something short and indelicate upon it. She crawls beneath the covers. The time is seven thirty-four. Remi sleeps.

Aggie wakes.

The first thing she does is stretch, languorously, unworried that the movement might disturb her slumbering partner. The second thing she does is check the writing-pad. There is a message, inscribed in painfully neat print. The message reads:

> Out of milk. Cabbage is fascinating. I love you. Very productive day.

She conceals a smile, and wriggles out of bed, pushing cold toes into protesting slippers. Tuesdays are her nights off, so she's in no hurry. Breakfast (or perhaps she should call it dinner?) is a lazy affair; she finds pasta in the cupboard and a tub of bolognese sauce in the microwave. There's no milk, but there's juice and green tea. The corner store opens at six-thirty and closes at seven, so she won't be able to buy groceries until winter, when the days are shorter and her nights are longer. Aggie writes a note saying 'MILK' and pins it to the fridge, pointedly.

There's no leftover paperwork for her to fuss over, so she curls up on the sofa with a mug of tea and a book she's been meaning to read for a while. It's a good book; not her usual genre, but Remi recommended it for her, and she knows by now to trust Remi's instincts. She keeps a small notebook beside her. As Aggie reads, she jots down small observations. In a particularly thrilling part, she writes down nothing at all, absorbed in the action, mouth hanging slightly open. When the chapter reaches its climax she lets out a sharp exhale and writes half a line of exclamation marks. By the end of the chapter her tea has grown cold.

The book occupies her for a pleasant few hours. It has a relaxing effect on her, akin to the feeling of a long massage on a warm day, or the feeling of floating in a deserted sea, salt lapping at her ankles, surrounded by horizon. After she has finished it the effect remains, and she sighs and wriggles her toes.

Midnight falls. Aggie has six hours and twenty-three minutes left. Something crackles beneath her, and she staves off an intense feeling of deja vu. She reaches for the crackling thing, and finds a crumpled receipt, with something written on the back of it in Remi's neat handwriting. The writing reads:

> What if all kitchenware was sentient? Society as we know it? Cutlery????

An undignified giggle bursts from her lips, and she covers her mouth. After so many years she has grown adept at interpreting Remi's seemingly nonsensical offerings. She leaves them strewn about the house like leaves, or dying butterflies. This one is an idea. Aggie wonders what Remi was doing when she thought of it.

There are fourteen little notes scattered about since she last went hunting for them. Half are story ideas; the other half are of a more personal nature.

The personal messages read like this:

I love you, lumpy.

In another life I am your constant companion in waking. We frequently take leisurely strolls through the park and you may look into my eyes whenever you wish. In sleep we twine together like limpets. You are a very attractive limpet.

My love for you is a mnemonic. My love for you is a pirate ship. I have been thinking about the adventures that we might have had or will have.

There are two buckets in Remi's cupboard (study); one is marked 'LOVE' and the other 'WORK'. Aggie sorts the notes into piles and relocates them appropriately. It wouldn't do to lose them to the vacuum cleaner, after all. When she is done she slumps back into the battered sofa, suddenly exhausted. A thought strikes her. It's a thought she has had many times before. It goes: would it be easier to pursue a lover who was not diurnal, but nocturnal, like herself? She inspects and dissects the thought, as she has before, and comes to the same conclusion that she always has. (Which is, of course: yes, and, in so very many ways, no.)

After a while Aggie rouses herself, and returns to the living room. Outside the window the darkness is a tangible thing. It presses against the glass like an old friend, and she acknowledges it silently, pressing the tip of one finger to the window-pane. She has four hours left until sunrise. She can feel the weariness seeping into her bones.

There is a particular character arc that Remi has been wrestling with over the past week. Yesternight Aggie had an idea that she thinks will solve the problem. It's a knotty problem, though, so she can't say for sure. Still, she makes another pot of green tea, and writes down her idea, making sure to write down all of the thoughts that led to it, and some thoughts that might spring from it.

When she is done she checks her watch. The time is one past six.

Aggie finishes her tea and washes the mug in the sink. She showers and brushes her teeth and walks into the bedroom. There is a pad of paper on the bedside table. She writes a message. The time is six twenty-three.

She falls asleep, clutching the hand of her partner, who wakes up just as the sun rises from the distant east. Remi reaches for the pad of paper.

Today Remi will remember to buy milk and she will sort out a gnarly character arc. She will write sixteen messages, twelve for love and four for work. Tonight Aggie will fleck the sleeves of her scrubs with blood, and have to wait until morning to change clothes.

The day after tomorrow one of the ducks will escape and Remi will have to chase it about the streets in her dressing-gown, barefoot. The night after tomorrow night Aggie will write about how much she loves her, and she will do the same the night after, and all the nights after that.

For now, the sun is brightening.

In Weather Like This

Joel Mak

Rain tap dancing on car hoods. All the ink coming off the sheets of rain-soaked paper taped to lamp poles on the street, their histories erased: subletting adverts, garage sale notices, guitar lessons, Marxist colloquiums, 'Have you seen?'s, and the like. Buses roaring down their lanes – aggressors of the night – their radiators spouting machine-gun poetry, straying dangerously close to the sidewalks and sending up waves avoided by pedestrians brandishing umbrellas with broken spokes. Young women running across roads with books over their heads. Uncollected laundry hanging off Hills Hoists, invisible men reaching for the floor. Pots overflowing with water sitting on balconies housing dead leafless plants.

Lost seagulls deep in suburbia, just outside the cover of petrol stations, fat drops of water landing like mortar shells on their feathered heads and you wonder if it bothers them. Homeless men tucked in their sleeping bags on George Street, dead to the world. Traffic lights swaying in concerto with the trees. Bicycles waiting for their owners, leaning sadly against signposts. Water rising in lidless trashcans. Drivers in stalled traffic, drumming their steering wheels, watching the windscreen wipers. Commuters looking up from their mobile phones and out the window when the train rushes out of a tunnel into the stormy night.

In weather like this it's guaranteed that there's someone somewhere standing under an awning. Static silhouettes of men, one hand balled up in the pouches of their coats, another holding an umbrella, just like real-life shots of a Brett Amory painting. Men standing in the Friday post-work hours of suburban Sydney where the shops are closed save for that one convenience store. Men waiting for that relief, for that period of dryer rain, if such a thing exists at all, to tackle the next block then the next; men en route home, thinking of the hum of microwave ovens, of the weekend footy, of their partners dreaming on vinyl couches.

There's a three-car pile-up somewhere, an accident being reported on the radio of the South Asian storekeeper. Traffic's slowed to a crawl on the M4 because that's exactly what it's slowed down to. In weather like this he always thinks of: green curry cooking on the stove, guarded like a national treasure by his mother and the childhood smell of his father's coat after he came home from work. There's the jingle followed by the radio jockey's mellow but booming voice saying something about how he hopes all commuters are taking it easy on the road, it sure looks feisty out there, but not to worry because he's got Jim Croce and Kenny Rogers coming up to accompany the weather-trodden on this frightful Friday night. From upstairs there's the sound of music coming from a cheap pair of speakers, chairs scraping against wooden floorboards as people get up or sit down. Conversations, anecdotes, jokes.

Middle of the second half and the spectators are soaked and/or bored. Parramatta would have been slugging it out with Manly all night long, the score 6–4 to Parramatta, plus Jamie Lyon of Manly missing the one he never misses, failing to convert from practically right in front of the posts and they've slow-motioned that kick to oblivion, telling the audience to just wait for it, watch exactly when Lyon's standing boot starts to slide under him as his kicking boot's about to come in contact with the ball, the grass just not standing up to the punishment the weather's dishing out.

On formal first dates you're lucky if the weather's like this; a heaven-sent icebreaker, something to laugh about at first eye-contact with your date without a word being exchanged, in the waiting area of some restaurant on Darling Harbour. You couldn't stop thinking about her the past week and now she's here; before the first hello you can hear rain battering the pavement, Vivaldi on the stereo, forks and knives on ceramic plates, and the low rumble of polite chatter.

* * *

The storekeeper has a habit of sniffling whenever someone walks in and triggers the buzzer: that contraption installed way back in ninety-eight now sounds like a cat with a scratchy throat; the sniffle a way of letting the customer know someone's in the quiet store. When the hooded teenager comes in drenched to the bone, the storekeeper only thinks of the fact that he's forgotten to move the umbrella rack to the entrance.

They've even slow-mo'd the look on Lyon's face prior to the kick. They're saying that's the look of a troubled player in the middle of stalled contract talks, a player whose head just isn't in it. One presenter saying that it's the whole Origin selection fiasco, telling his two co-presenters that mate, if Lyon doesn't wanna play Origin then he doesn't wanna play Origin mate, why would you pick someone who doesn't wanna play? Plus the obligatory slow mo. of the reaction after the kick too: Lyon's hands on hips, head pulled back looking at the heavens which've opened up tonight, his team mates behind the goal line looking on blank-faced though there are one or two with hung heads – they know every point matters in weather like this.

With most women you notice what they're wearing, then you notice the way they laugh, though you only really fall in love when you register what they laugh at. We talked the work week, family members and classical music. I told her I dug Handel even though I think all Handel sounds like an incredibly long walk down the aisle during a marriage ceremony and you're not even the groom. We talked Darling Harbour, gelato, and Europe. Every woman shakes their heads and laughs after being posed the question: who'd you shag, kill, and marry out of Pitt, Clooney, and DiCaprio?

* * *

Half the people that walk into convenience stores in weather like this just want to get dry. Storekeepers don't mind because most of them end up making a guilty purchase. Hip hop seeps out the headphones of the teenager, his wet runners painting patches on the dirty cement floor. From upstairs there's random bursts of laughter indicating the type of party where multiple small groups have formed, each one leading a different conversation. The South Asian man likes this Croce tune about one hand on the bible and the other on a gun.

Some teams, knowing that the weather's going to be foul on game day, hose the balls down with water while they train during the week. Nothing doing, today: knock-ons, overthrown passes, kicks landing on the full, loose grips. The commentators are still talking about Jamie Lyon. They're saying that what distinguishes a first-class football player from a squad player is that the first-class player has already forgotten the miss, urging Lyon who cannot possibly hear that if he is in fact a top quality player to prove it, mate. A cameraman's caught footage of some spectator pulling out a steaming sausage from his thermos with a pair of chopsticks. You can see water collecting on the empty blue fibre glass seats. That fan in the background can't even wave the flag because it's too darn heavy.

She told me that she used to own this djellaba which she bought in a Moroccan market, a perfect snuggie for this kind of weather. The djellaba had to go to an op-shop after she moved houses; everyone's got a habit of accumulating stuff we can't possibly take with us all our lives. My eyes on hers the entire time yet I knew she was shifting her feet under the table like an anxious child. Most people take ages to answer the question: if you could listen in on a conversation between two dead people with the exception of Jesus Christ, who would they be? You think Cobain, you think Hendrix, and you wonder what they'd even wanna talk about.

* * *

In weather like this in some over-lit store there's an old lady fumbling for change, plastic bags hanging off both arms, one hand holding onto an umbrella that's dripping wet. The ceiling is high and business slow. The young employee slides a mop in circular arcs on linoleum floor up and down aisles. This convenience store's as cramped and compact as convenience stores can be. The fluorescent lighting is dim. Tom T. Hall sings about how he got to Memphis. The ceiling is low and it's business as usual. The teenager ambles up and down the two aisles, eyes going over the labels of goods; the storekeeper looking out the entrance into the night, at the falling rain illuminated by car headlights.

In weather like this beer served at stadiums tastes like water. Attendance today is in the low ten thousands. No one wants to start or join a Mexican wave. Security usher with wet scarves around their necks, fleece vests under their fluorescent vests, controlling a crowd that's not going to get out of control. The Sea Eagle mascot's trudging around the stadium flapping its wings and all everyone can think about is how the kid in the costume's dry and warm. The commentators are already talking about next week's big, huge, prime-time, absolutely pivotal match while players are packing in a scrum for the third time. You can see mud and grass caked between the studs of football boots.

I overheard the waitress at reception talking about cancelled reservations with her manager, giving him a 'what can you do' shrug. My date told me she used to do ballet when she was a kid, up till about year nine or ten. She was lead in a show set to *The Nutcracker* suite. Said she remembers seeing her mother in the audience, sitting next to an empty seat reserved for her father and that it was pouring like today because in the third act her dad came in looking like he'd taken a shower fully clothed, came down the middle aisle looking for his place, distracting everyone, like a Robinson Crusoe who'd finally made it home.

* * *

The radio jockey repeats the names of the songs he's just put on, mentions something about a tree on a street in a suburb you've never heard of. Says it really is no joke, tells listeners to be careful out there folks, to stay indoors if you can, have a hot chocolate by the telly instead. The storekeeper thinks of his wife giving a bath to his two year old son. Nothing like soaking yourself in warm water in weather like this. The buzz of conversations getting louder and louder upstairs as people try to make themselves heard over themselves.

Three minutes from time and a beauty of a ball is kicked deep into Parramatta territory where Jarryd Hayne's the only player around. Tracking back, running into the condensation of his own breath he can feel the purple and white jerseys coming in on him, fingers pointing that way and this way, players calling their markers. Men and their sons in oversized team jerseys stand under transparent raincoats, shivering, the excitement of game day dissipating by the minute. Spectators walk up or down the stairs, heading for the exits. The commentators had a laugh when their directors told them to put on footage some cameraman caught of a bored five-year-old spectator blowing his nose into a tissue, then proceeding to look at what he'd produced like it was a high-level maths problem.

When she was a kid she used to run her fingers underneath cold metal railings, letting the water run between them. Her rain music of choice being Tomasz Stańko, Davis's input for *Ascenseur pour L'échafaud*, and, she laughs here, Bob Marley. She has said that her dream was to one day open her own op-shop, an op shop-come-café with two huge bookshelves on one side of the wall so it'd be like an op shop-come-café-come-bookstore, really. She'd name the place *Shelter From The Storm* and like I said, we fall in love when we get the references.

* * *

Young adults smoking cigarettes and drinking red wine on covered balconies. All men put their free hand in their pockets while the other holds their beverage. There's alcohol spilled everywhere of course. Amoebic patches of liquid not unlike those on benches in the bus shelter just across the street. Downstairs the storekeeper's dialing triple zero: someone ran off with a fistful of cash after he forced the storekeeper to open the till, the scoundrel's hand darting for the yellow shades, a quick nervous grab knocking the till over and there's money scattered everywhere. Barry Manilow telling whoever's listening that he wrote the songs that make the whole world sing.

Hayne sprints back, taking one quick look behind him as he runs towards the ball that's landed just inside his team's goal line, the closest incoming Sea Eagle slowing down with fatigue this late in the game. The ball rocks on the grass like an egg ready to hatch; Hayne scoops it like an eagle does its prey, then jams his right foot in front of him and turns right back around, a graceful one-eighty. There's an abandoned beach ball on ground level where kids're chasing each other, jumping over cones and railings.

After dinner, walking past the Chinese Gardens we both noticed the young women walking with caution, their heels looking for islands of dry pavement to walk on, hugging their purses close to their chests. Her hand on my forearm as I walked her to her car, our heads close together, ducked under our umbrella like soldiers in a field of war.

* * *

The teenager, huffing and puffing, strides as long as he can. Someone told him once that if you think you're going to slip, that's exactly what you're gonna do, so he doesn't think about it. The earphones no longer in his ear, the wires flailing this way and that way. Two, three blocks away now. Once you're out of earshot of the victim screaming HEY HEYYY!, once you're out of the zone where people might notice, then you're home free babe, all bases touched. But he keeps running anyway, with his head down like he's running to stay dry, rather than head up like he's running to stay out of bars, running past couples under umbrellas who don't register his existence at all, way deep in whispered conversation.

Blink and you miss it. The fatigued Sea Eagle runs towards Hayne, both of them hugging the sideline. Hayne has to come back inside: it's what you're coached to do: come back inside or they'll gang up on you in no time and you're giving back the ball on the one or two, 6-4 to us but they've got four, five goes for the try. And the Sea Eagle knows that Hayne's got to come back in, he's dropped his left shoulder, ready to engage, wet hair in his eyes but he can make out Hayne making the logical move; there's the natural brace, the tensing of the lats, but no impact. Hayne's shoulder's gone inside but his legs have brought him slightly back towards his own goal line, maybe even knowing that the Sea Eagle will fall forward or even slip into the tackle rather than stand him up and the Sea Eagle does fall, grasps at the air near Hayne's shorts – you could've been the hero and now someone else is man – and Hayne sees five metres ahead of him: everywhere a curtain of rain but all green grass, spotlights bright up above.

If there's a time for cigarettes it's when you're with a woman in a stationary car. The engine's killed, the radio's off so you can listen to nature's soundtrack. It's all information. One soul-revealing item after another: how someone uses the visor for cards and receipts; whether or not someone keeps a box of tissues in the glove box; the type of air freshener. And everyone compares these new details to the last woman or man, not so much as lingering reminders of past romances but memories sending out that last dying signal before they're to be replaced by new ones forging now. New information's better information.

* * *

The teenager's ten blocks away. His hood's off his head and he's counted the crumpled cash and it's worth something to him of course but to the Herald probably a paragraph and nothing more. They'll say something about a young man of — appearance, off with $— into the dark. The newspaper won't mention the rain because they believe it doesn't matter, but no one ever thinks twice about people running in weather like this.

In the post-game commentary everyone's forgotten about Lyon. Parramatta 12–4. They're pointing out how Hayne's the type of player who only needs five metres of space to compute where and how he's going to run and with a sidestep and acceleration like that in weather like this? Mate. They're saying that in weather like this, on a night like tonight, it needed something special to seal the deal and that something special came from the Hayne Train and look at him, celebrating with the Hayne Plane. They're saying that Hayne delivered what the loyal rugby league spectators paid their money to see: genius, chutzpah, flair, freakish talent. Cue footage of celebrating Parramatta players, wet muscular bodies in blue and gold, singing in the rain.

It might be cold and wet or we might be dry and sweaty the day we've got no more information to pass on, nothing left to give, everything to learn already learned, bodies and souls bared, layerless. Or that day might not come at all. Diverging paths, difference in opinion, a slip of the tongue. But tonight: a peck on the cheek, signaling that she's more than willing to try. No, there's nothing like winning in the rain.

Aturan Main

Tamasin Young

Aturan Main
Adilkah ini?

Semerbak bau wangi cengkeh
menarikku
sepangjang aliran asap
tak ada aturan main
taka da garis lurus
di pulau lurus

Tetapi untuk mencari ketidakberatan hati
di antara perjuangan orang lain
Adilkah ini?

Rules of the Game

Translation by Tamasin Young

The rules of the game.
Are they fair?

The smell of cloves
pulls me
along the line of smoke;
there are no rules of the game
there are no straight lines
on this straight island.

But to find this weightlessness
amongst other people's struggles:
is that fair?

The Killer's Postcard is Missing

Zenobia Wilde

Announcer

And now we present the final instalment of Renée Niz's adaptation of Agatha Christie's *The Killer's Postcard is Missing*, starring Bertram Oak as Miss Marple.

[Increasingly dramatic music plays.]

To recap briefly on the story so far:

Sir Stanley Blade has been found poisoned in his study. An hour before he had played host to an aggressive group of merchant bankers, of whom only Elbert Waddington still remains in the country. Sir Stanley's daughter, Miss Patricia Blade, hopes to marry Mr Fredrick Slide, ne'er-do-well biological son of the late Edgar Pourout, and adopted son of Lord Compute. Meanwhile, Lord Bountiful's adulterous affair with Mrs Stella Bloke has been exposed by her husband, Mr Roger Bloke. Mr Bloke was acting as secretary to a wealthy American businessman who has since disappeared after securing the sum of £3000 from Sir Stanley in suspicious circumstances. Lady Edging has been seen at the theatre twice now with Lord Braithwaite, giving desperately needed substance to society gossip, but as they've nothing to do with this story, we can forget about them. Miss Patricia's secret wedding to Mr Slide has brought an end to their engagement but may cause more problems with her aunt, Madame Denie, who is back in the country after an absence of sixteen years, following the death of her husband under possibly suspicious circumstances in Paris last April. Sir Stanley's neighbour, meanwhile – the apparently harmless Miss Olger Spinster – has been found dead by knife-wound and her entire house has been stolen. Her nephew and heir, Mr Robin Abank, has appeared after many years of mysterious absence, bringing with him a Mr Philip Roof. Mr Abank has spent the last two episodes insisting that they are just good friends, but Mrs Nosey, who runs the pub down the road, suspects there is something more going on. Not that she has any space to hurl stones, as it's been found out that both she and her husband were having separate affairs with Sir Stanley's cook, the widowed Mrs Blank. Miss Marple has just arranged for all the suspects to gather in Sir Stanley's office.

And if all that sounds confusing, well, you should have been paying more attention, you lazy bastard.

[Opening music plays.]

Narrator
Agatha Christie's *The Killer's Postcard is Missing*; adapted for radio by Renée Niz and starring Bertram Oak as Miss Marple; episode thirty-seven thousand, five hundred and fifty-one.

[Sounds of general milling as suspects enter the room.]

Patricia
Freddie!

Fredrick
Yes, Pat?

Patricia
Not a word, remember? Not. A. Word.

Fredrick
Oh yes. Absolutely. Silence on all fronts. With you, Pat darling.

Patricia
[Exasperated sigh.]
[General chatter again.]

Madame Denie
[With bad French accent.] Ah, Monsieur Abank. How are you today?

Robin
Well, thank you, Madame. [Lowering voice] I say, you don't know what all this is about, do you?

Madame Denie

What do you mean? [Without accent] That's not in the script!

Robin

I know, but I'm darned confused. Why have we all been herded into this room?

Madame Denie

[Without accent.] This is the final scene, you fluff-brain! The detective is about to make the final accusation.

Robin

Like in Cluedo?

Madame Denie

What?

Robin

You know, Cluedo. The board game. The whole process of 'I think Professor Green did it in the dining room with the candlestick' and all that sort of thing.

Madame Denie

Yes, yes. Fine. Like in Cluedo, yes. Now, could we please get back to the script?

Robin

Right-o.
[General chatter again, which then dies down.]

Miss Marple

Hello everyone. I'd like first to thank you all for meeting me here, in Sir Stanley's office.

Patricia

Do you know who the killer is, then, Miss Marple?

Miss Marple

Indeed I do, Patricia. But before I tell you, I'm going to make several barely-relevant observations and tell a long and winding story before seeming to accuse each of you in turn.

Robin
Perhaps we could skip all that then. It'll save time.

Miss Marple
That's not a bad idea, Robin. We'll get to lunch faster that way.
[Pause.] Page ninety-three, then.
[Sound of many pages being turned.]

Fredrick
It was a very long story, then.

Miss Marple
Oh yes. It would have been marvellous.
Ah, here we go. Right. [Clears throat.]
First I must ask you, Mr Slide, what you were doing in London with
Miss Blade on Thursday.

Fredrick
Ah, well, now …

Patricia
Oh, for god's sake, Freddie. She obviously knows. We were getting
married, Miss Marple.
[Vague shocked noises about the room.]

Miss Marple
[Knowingly.] Yes, yes, I thought so.

Fredrick
But what has that got to do with Sir Stanley's death? Or Miss
Spinster's?

Miss Marple
Oh, nothing really. It's my job, you see, to expose those secrets
which would have come out in a year or two anyway. I rather enjoy
it. So now we move on to Madame Denie.

Madame Denie
Ye – ah. Oui?

Miss Marple

I began to wonder about you when I first saw you sign your name. The handwriting seemed strangely familiar. And then I placed it. The hand that signed your name was the same hand that wrote Sir Stanley's suicide note.

[Gasps from all. The sound of a chair being pulled back as Madame Denie stands up.]

Madame Denie

I have had enough of this.

Miss Marple

Madame, please sit down and let me finish explaining –

Madame Denie

[Losing accent.] No, no. I have had it. You cannot accuse moi! I didn't sign up for a murder mystery, you know. I wanted to be Lady Macbeth.

There's a pause.

Miss Marple

You know, in a way, *Macbeth* is a murder mystery.

Madame Denie

[Totally without accent.] Oh, balls.

[Opening music plays again, more dramatically, with variation.]

Madame Denie

[Melodramatically, in the voice of Lady Macbeth.] Out, damned spot! Out, I say! One, two. Why then 'tis time to do't. Hell is murky. Fie, my lord, fie, a soldier, and afeard? What need we fear? Who knows it, when none can call our power to account? Yet who would have thought the old man to have had so much blood in him?

Miss Marple

Yes. I rather thought it was you.

Madame Denie

[Still dramatically and in the voice of Lady Macbeth.] How was I exposed?

Miss Marple
I've been speaking to your husband.

Madame Denie
How dare he speak against me! What did he say?

Miss Marple
'Is this a dagger I see before me,
the handle towards my hand?'
It was quite clear you had drugged him, which is why he's been
absent from the story all this time. You've kept him in the
cupboard.

Madame Denie
[Confused.] The cupboard … ?
[Opening music plays, again, with more variation; less drama, more
daytime infomercial.]

Miss Marple/Presenter
And what are the chances of being trapped in a cupboard by a
loved one?
Well, it may surprise some, but the statistics are rising. Over two
people were put in cupboards last year by their spouses, up from
point three people the previous year. And these figures do not
include those shoved quickly into cupboards by those they're
sleeping with because their spouse's just come home. Later on, we'll
be talking to Ms Francis Drake about her time in a cupboard two
years ago but now –

Madame Denie
No. No, no, no. Stop. This is getting far too ridiculous.

Miss Marple
Oh. I rather liked that one.
[A bell rings.]

Cross.art

Dover Dubosarsky

Across	**Down**
4 Words (3)	1 To look (2)
6 Permute (3)	2 Is to waste (3)
7 Change (2)	3 Stop (3)
8 Revert (3)	5 Give up (3)
9 Life (3)	9 Now (3)
10 Becomes (2)	12 The game (3)
11 Work (3)	14 Is (3)
13 Pain (3)	15 Over (2)

Comic Endings

Gabriella Edelstein

I desperately fear and yet I yearn for a comic ending, with jazz
music and a three-tiered cake, wrapped up forever after with a gold
band. Yet, that ring will encircle my
tongue and masticate my words. I will be silenced by a modern
scold's bridle,
made beautiful with a diamond crust. Will I, a tamed shrew, be
allowed an
ironic epilogue? Or will I stand there silent, for good measure,
while I
am girdled by the play? As life goes on there shall be a shudder and
a gasp, a call and a closing, and then a gaping quiet. For who
will respond to a whisper of discontent? A call in the night
for freedom, for desire, for escape from the four-
bedroom, two-bathroom enclosure will go
unanswered. Yet, I dream, Someday My
Prince Will Come. Though once he
does, will anyone want to hear me
sing? No, they don't tell you the
greatest tragedy for women is
the comic ending. Where
once there was a voice,
soon there will be
nothing but
silence.

Peter and Laura

Troy Wong

You want to know what I think really happened?
Why, because I'm his brother? Does this somehow make my story
more reliable than yours?
Or is it because you think I know something you don't?
You've read his poems, haven't you? You think there's got to be
more to it.
Well, you'd be right to think so.
But it's nothing like you're probably hoping for.
Look, Peter never said anything that'd change the jury's verdict. But
what he told me did change what I told myself to make sense of the
whole mess.
It all started in a church. Peter looks across the room and sees her.

* * *

I

At first sight, I was no longer my own.
Her golden hair that fell in perfect place,
her ice-blue eyes that shattered time and space;
when they met mine – every colour and tone
around us blurring, senses overthrown
by simply knowing of her presence there,
so close and yet so far – were but a snare.
To me, like sirens beckoning me home.
And so, in such a fleeting glance, my fate
was sealed. 'Til death I was forever bound
to her; a stranger flooding through my heart
by chance, whose dreadful beauty made me hate
the things that I'd once loved, in whole and part;
my other idle gods were, by her, drowned.
It's love at first sight. The enduring classic.
But there's a problem. She's wearing a wedding ring.

IV

The coming week was black: a haze of pains,
from dullest pangs to murderous, stabbing aches
inside my ribcage. Breathing seemed to take
all effort: in and out and in again.
I knew my old self vaguely, much like trains
speeding past platforms as furious grey ghosts
leave but an image while all else is lost,
or as a raincloud broadcasts coming rains.
But ah! The sweetness of my agony!
I cursed my life, yet found no joy in death,
for deep in sleep of death I'd have no hope
that love would come to cure my malady
at last, some distant day 'til which I'll mope,
asphyxiating, counting every breath.

* * *

Weeks pass. Then one week, he finds the courage to go up to her.
Maybe it's just a quick conversation; maybe not. Maybe her
husband was with her; maybe he wasn't. I don't know. To be honest
with you, I don't think even he remembers that far back.
What I do know is, that was the night he learned her name.
Laura.
Maybe he repeats the name under his breath, on the way home, in
the shower. Sings it, sighs it. Says it with a smile and a laugh. Maybe
he mouths the word like a prayer before bed.
Laura.
Laura.
Laura.

* * *

XII

Ah, Laura! Laura's the name on my heart,
written in ink on every rippling vein,
tattooed to my soul and marked in my brain
like sacred law. And so I'm set apart

from every other living being. I start
my life anew tonight: this blessed time's
preserved forever in my racing mind,
'til I, from this round earth, at last depart.
Yes! Laura's the name on my lips and tongue;
I mouth the words and taste the holy sound
that spills from holy instruments entwined
in orgiastic ecstasy. All's sung
in burning fervour: 'Praise the Lord!', I'm blind
with adoration; see, my love's unbound!

XIII

My love for her grows like all-climbing vines
slowly assailing the waning walls
of an old building, creeping through the halls
and places where people once lived their lives;
forming green networks and vegetable lines
down derelict brickwork and dusty floors,
peeking through windows, prying open doors
so that no space or locked room can survive
uninvaded. Its roots dig deeper down,
through the loamy earth beneath the building,
wrapping round cornerstones to drink their strength
'til they crumble, and crack the ground
on which the whole sprawling structure depends.
The house hunches; soon, the walls will cave in.

* * *

Of course, learning her name's not enough for him. He's got to have
her.
But first, he's got to get rid of the husband – a man named Jared.
There's another churchgoer, a woman named Jane. He gets to know
her well enough to find out that, lucky for him, she's secretly in love
with the husband.
He's got a plan, and he starts making moves right away. Starts
dropping hints to Laura, starts making suggestions. Plays with her
mind. Makes her suspect Jared's up to no good.

A few weeks later, he goes to a church dinner party at Laura and Jared's place. It's winter. They're rugged up; they've got the fireplace going. Jane's there too.

* * *

XIX

I think I see a fire burning green
within her eyes as they reflect the flame,
which, all the while, stay focused on the same
one target: Jared, Laura, each unseen
to all but Jane and I, arranged between
our present circumstances and our goal,
who both blockade and yet, evince the whole
of all we've thirsted for in daytime dreams.
'I know you want a drink,' I say to Jane.
'I don't,' she says; I pour one anyway
And tell her, 'Try to quell your love for now;
enjoy yourself! A drink will ease your pain'
– as well as common sense, and so allow
hidden passions to see the light of day.

XX

'Why suppress the pain of love,' she returns,
'when bitter pleasure's nestled there as well?
I wish for no relief from this hot hell;
in fact, I nurse this flame so I may burn.'
'But burning's all you do,' I say. 'You've yearned
for him so long, as deep-sea divers ache
for breath they need for life, but cannot take
until back to the surface they're adjourned.
So drink with me this glass, and more, and more,
'til heavy inhibition leaves you be;
then, make your move upon your joy, your grief;
the distant one you worship and adore.'
And so convinced, she drinks 'til Laura leaves
the scene; then, Jane sets forth for all to see.

XXI

Suddenly she throws herself upon him,
drunken and groping, cooing epithets
in love and longing, making clear she's set
her heart upon him, her hands on his skin,
roaming to take account of foreign things:
the roughness of his palms, his solid waist,
the prickling shapes of stubble on his face,
and last, the startling softness of his lips –
then Laura reappears, and thinking Jane
the perpetrator of this thought-out crime
with Jared as her co-conspirator,
throws herself upon them both, in pain
of heartbreak, screaming every damning slur
and cursing them feverishly, 'whore!' and 'swine!'

* * *

Laura gets herself so worked up, she has an asthma attack. The mad
rush for her ventilator somewhat distracts people from getting
caught up in the real chaos: Jared, poor bastard, embarrassed half
to death. Jane, probably spewing in some corner.
Now, don't ask me why Jared never denied anything; it's a mystery
to me. Hah, maybe he was sleeping around after all.
Anyway, they split not long after.
And not long after that, Peter starts seeing Laura.

* * *

XXIII

I love her as a soldier loves his sword
on the field of battle, when enemies
form charging ranks in foreign territories,
and nothing's left to do but face the horde.
I love her as a servant loves his lord,
weak and subservient, dependent on him
for food and shelter, subject to his whim,
with every breath allowed by his accord.

And yet I labour: hear the woman's moans
In agony of childbirth as she strains
to deliver our lovely consummation.
It seems as well that all creation groans
as I groan for the day the complication
of my love's gone, and I'm freed from my chains.

* * *

One night she takes him to these cliffs beside the ocean. Very
secluded area; hardly any streetlights; stars, moon, very romantic.
They leave the car somewhere and take a long walk.

Peter doesn't know at the time that these cliffs were where Jared
proposed to Laura. I can only guess why Laura might've taken him
there.

So they're walking – Peter told me they must've been maybe two
hundred metres from the car – when suddenly they hear windows
smashing and the car alarm going off.

Peter runs back and sees a guy with a baseball bat smashing his
vehicle. Jared. He's reaching in through the windows and pulling
out everything he can find – bags, CD's, books, jumpers – and
throwing it all over the cliff and into the waves.

* * *

XXXV

I run fast to him, thirsting for a fight;
he turns and sees me, roars a lion's roar
and swings; I dodge; we stumble 'cross the floor,
both scrambling for the weapon, pitting might
and hand; he seizes on the bat; locked tight
on one another's bodies, clothing rips;
inflamed, I wrench the bat from iron grips
and beat him, dealing fatal blows outright.
enough. I watch a shape of blood crawl slow
across the concrete from beneath his head,
his body shaking like a brainless thing:
just muscle, signals, movement, broken bones:

a warrior defeated, downed in the ring
for the scavenger birds, so left for dead.

* * *

The coroner reported that Jared died from 'repeated blows to the
head with a blunt metal object' – his own baseball bat.
Laura's standing there watching all of this unfold.
She has another asthma attack.
But this time, she doesn't have her ventilator.

* * *

XXXVII

I rush to her and beg, to no avail.
'My ventilator' – all she strains to gasp –
'but all our bags and things inside are cast
into the waves and sea below!' I wail,
and so I sprint out to the road to hail
a passing stranger, but find none at all;
'A phone!' I think, but cannot make a call,
for mine and Laura's phones did also sail
straight through the air into the crashing sea,
and Jared's, when I double back to check
his cooling corpse, is smashed to toothy shards.
I kneel by Laura, praying she be free
at once from Panic's grip which chokes her hard,
but fail. I know I've only one choice left.

XXXVIII

I meet the cliff's edge, heave a breath, and leap
into nothing, find the darkness below
myself and fall, the seconds crawling slow
through my brain 'til the water meets my feet.
With a crash I slice into the rough sea's
rolling black metal skin. The shock of cold –
the ocean swallows me, hauls me slow
against my fearful, frenzied flailing, deep

into its hidden bowels. The panic fast
tears from my desperate lungs the hard-held air;
I flail and kick myself up to the clear
for a second, splutter and choke and gasp
on a wave before I'm pulled back down, mere
and weak against the god who holds me there.

* * *

They told me he was stone-cold when they dragged him from the
water.
Even after they'd beaten the life back into him and he'd coughed
and spat out the ocean from his lungs, even after the warm
towels and all those nights handcuffed to his hospital bed and the
counseling sessions, he looked like a dead man.
Early on, the media didn't really know how to spin the story. Most
of the news reports told it like a murder mystery. But one of them
tried to frame it like a love story: 'man jumps into ocean to retrieve
asthmatic lover's ventilator'.
Sounds romantic, don't you think?
But one night in the hospital, when the hallways were quiet and the
other patients were asleep, Peter told me the truth.
He didn't jump off that cliff with any grand delusions of finding
Laura's bag with her ventilator in it, not in time to save her, and
not from the waves in pitch black darkness. Believe me, he had no
intentions of finding anything down there.
Here's the secret:
Peter can't swim.

* * *

XL

Pitiful creature of desperate desire,
chasing shafts of sunlight through the cold caves
it was born in, a poor addict who craves
the old escape, a kite, aching for higher
flight but lacking winds and meeting tired
breezes instead, which skips and flutters weakly

for a moment before descending meekly
to haggard earth, only to then expire –
at last we've reached the truth. Reality's
a hard, unyielding thing, hear me: we ape
contentedness, when all the while we strain
after empty dreams and idle deities
despite our collected façade – our pain
can never heal, but only change its shape.

Complaints Department

Evelyn Araluen Corr

Colin wasn't very sure what he was doing. He looked up at the intimidating building in front of him and made a small huffing noise. No one seemed to hear him, and in truth he didn't want anyone to hear him because it might cause a scene and he absolutely detested scenes – but he was not, by nature, a hoverer, and he wasn't really sure how else his body could occupy the quiet London street if not by expressing quiet huffs that spoke of inconvenience and annoyance. He had a niece, Caitlin, who was absolutely wonderful at hovering – she stood in corners with an iPhone in hand and ignored everyone and everything around her. Colin didn't have an iPhone.

So he stepped towards the building and huffed a little louder – hoping the busy Londoners walking past would just assume he was one of them, forced to take time out of his busy schedule of sitting behind a desk and drinking coffee and going into intimidating buildings out of necessity alone. But he wasn't from London – he was from Cheshire, and he hated London. He was an accountant who managed the finances of several small businesses in his village, which allowed him to work from home most days, meaning his busy schedule was mostly comprised of sitting in his slippers while writing up the butcher's loan application, with occasional breaks to scratch behind his overweight cat's ears.

Colin wasn't in his slippers anymore, and he had left his overweight ginger tabby Mr Twiddleston at home to rifle through the neighbour's bins. He was smartly dressed, and he was still doing his best to look busy and important as he stepped into the foyer. There was a pleasant-looking receptionist sitting behind a desk, and two or three other men were sitting on a stylish but functionally useless settee, all looking as if they wanted to be at home with their cats and their slippers as well. He was just beginning to worry about how long he would be able to maintain his busy – and –

important-looking expression when the receptionist noticed him, and smiled invitingly.

'Hello, sir. May I help you?' she said brightly.

'Yes, hello, my name is Colin Patten and I received a letter about – '

'Oh, yes! Right you are, Mr Patten,' the young lady beamed. 'Mr Sparse and Mr Perkins have been waiting for you. If you would like to follow me … ' she said, bouncing up out of her chair with the enthusiasm of an individual who actually enjoyed their job. He felt like he had just seen a unicorn.

'The uh, letter I received wasn't very specific about what it is I'm actually doing here,' he said, following her after flashing a half apologetic, half triumphant smile to the three uncomfortable looking men still waiting on the settee.

'This is a complaints department, Mr Patten.'

'Yes but I haven't – I mean I haven't really got any – '

'In here, Mr Patten. Mr Sparse and Mr Perkins will be with you momentarily. Would you like some tea?' the woman chirped, pushing open a door to what looked like a small conference room.

'Uh, no, I think I'll be – '

'*Tea*, Maryanne!' suddenly came a loud, shrill voice.

'Right you are, Mr Sparse,' she said, stepping out into the hall as two men joined Colin in the room.

'Good morning, Mr Patten,' greeted a short, pale, waistcoated man in the same shrill voice. 'I do hope it wasn't an inconvenience for you to come all this way to meet with us?' he asked, stepping past without waiting for an answer. His tall, greyish companion followed silently, and immediately sat down.

'Well, actually, I had to take the train, and – '

'Marvellous! Where's Maryanne with that tea?' the waistcoated man demanded, even though the door had barely closed on the receptionist. 'Now, take a seat, Mr Patten, we have a lot to go through this morning.'

'Yes. Right. Well, alright,' Colin mumbled, sitting down as far away from the two gentlemen as he could without seeming rude.

'Marvellous, marvellous. Now, Mr Patten, my name is Sparse and this is my colleague Perkins here. Have you any idea where you are at the moment?' the waistcoated man began, placing a large briefcase on the conference table and snapping it open importantly. The greyish Perkins sat, still, large, looming and silent.

'Well, your receptionist said this was a – a complaints department?'

'And right she was! A complaints department is what we are, Mr Patten!' he said, trying to boom but instead squealing slightly. 'This is a unique organisation, developed to deal with the grievances and agonies of the ordinary, working class, reasonably educated, middle-aged men like you that are practically littering this fine country.'

Colin blinked. He was about to object before the receptionist bustled into the room with a laden tray, chiming 'Tea!'

'Tea! Tea, Mr Patten?' Sparse offered.

'Uh, tea – I mean, thank you,' he muttered, suddenly wishing he was sitting on the impractical settee in the foyer with all the other miserable people. He let Sparse's insults simmer slightly as the tea was poured, and wondered if the biannual trips to Madrid that his parents had taken him on as a child qualified him as being middle class.

'Thank you, Maryanne.'

'Thank you, Maryanne,' Colin repeated, and immediately regretted it when she replied with a wide smile as she excused herself. He grimaced in obligation. Perkins still sat quietly, looking absurdly comical as he raised his delicate floral teacup to his huge mouth with pinkie extended.

'She's an experiment that we're trialling, of course,' Sparse said, stirring one, two, three cubes of sugar into his tea.

'A what?' he exclaimed, experiencing sudden flashbacks to a gritty science fiction film his niece had forced him to watch.

'At the Bureau of Complaints and Grievances we aim to provide solutions for all the concerns facing mankind,' Sparse began grandly, leaning back in his chair and stirring the treacle that used to be his tea. 'Poor customer service is one of the most common complaints that we receive. We had Maryanne shipped over here from the United States, taught her to speak proper English and make a cup of tea, and what ho! We've not had a single problem since,' he said triumphantly. It was at this point that Colin decided Sparse was definitely the most bizarre person he had ever met, even more so than Caitlin's friend who smoked incense sticks and had once tried to put a spell on him when he said hello.

'I think that's actually a bit racist,' he frowned.

'Nonsense. Anyway, it's good to have some female presence here. Our services are, of course, aimed at men,' he continued.

'What about the women?'

'Oh, they usually just sort themselves out,' he brushed him off. 'Now, Mr Patten!' he began, as Colin tried to work out if that was sexist or not. 'Myself and my colleague are part of a subdivision of the BCG, sponsored by the Oxford English Dictionary Condensing Committee, and they have requested that we speak to you concerning a letter you wrote to your local paper on the fourth of July, 2012.'

'What on earth does that mean?'

'The OEDCC is a board of academics and public servicemen that was formed last year to condense the Oxford English Dictionary,' Sparse explained, plucking a photocopied sheet from out of his briefcase and passing it across to Colin as Perkins sipped his tea. He scanned it briefly, and recognised the three hundred or so words he had penned as part of his regular series of complaints featured in the *Cheshire Chronicle* last year.

'Well, I'm afraid I already have a pocket OED, and I don't see what my letter has to do with all this,' he said slowly, pushing the paper back to Sparse, who was now loudly slurping his tea.

'Oh no, Mr Patten! No, no, no! You aren't here to buy *dictionaries*, my good fellow!' he chuckled, but Colin wasn't feeling particularly good at all. 'No, we read your letter, Mr Patten, as part of our routine sweep of all small newspapers in this country, and we stumbled – '

'Wait, do you mean you actually *every* letter of complaint?'

'Only the ones that are posted, Mr Patten. Well, we read a lot that aren't. Well, we read a lot that aren't even – ' he stopped, and suddenly shared a surreptitious glance with Perkins, who was now nibbling on a macaroon. 'Yes, well – we're *very* in touch with the troubles of this great nation, Mr Patten,' he said smoothly. Colin wished he would stop saying *Mr Patten*, but he knew it would be much worse if he let the man call him Colin. 'And as such, we of course came across your letter about how much you despise people using too many flowery words to make themselves sound important,' he expounded. 'Now, we sent it off to the OEDCC, and they got back to us right away to say that you were *just* the sort of man they needed.'

'Needed for ... what?'

'Yes, Mr Patten – you are today's Englishman,' he began grandly, ignoring his question. 'You potter about in shops, stand in queues, complain about mortgages and write passive-aggressive letters to inconsequential newspapers – your vocabulary is limited but functional, and with the impending threat of a new, pan-English language, it is just your sort that we need to help us make some cuts,' he said, clasping his hands together as if waiting for applause from some unseen audience.

Colin thought carefully about his next sentence. 'You ... are insane.' But as much as he wanted to leave, curiosity made him stay.

'Not at all, Mr Patten!' Sparse cried, swinging around in his chair with the definite air of an insane man. 'I am merely a man trying to solve a problem, which you had the good character to point out to us here at the Bureau.'

'Yes, that's fine, but you are actually insane.'

'I am actually, certifiably not, I can assure you,' Sparse said smiling. Perkins poured himself a second cup of tea, and got started on what would be his third macaroon. 'You see, Mr Patten, what is *really* insane is writing endless complaints to trivial newspapers and not expecting anyone to do anything about it,' he said, wagging his finger in Colin's general direction.

'Well, I – I didn't even think anyone read those things!' he huffed.

'Madder still! Why, talking to yourself, even in the form of letters to your local paper is such a terrible waste of our precious, precious language!'

Colin picked up his teacup for the single purpose of putting it down noisily on the plate. 'Now, see here, I'm not – '

'We *are* willing to pay you for your services, Mr Patten.'

'Pay me to *what?*' he cried in exasperation.

'To provide us with the invaluable opinion of the average British citizen concerning the functionality of the modern English language, of course!' Sparse said, banging the table to emphasise his point. Perkins' tea cup rattled in its saucer.

'You mental bloody – are my taxes paying for people like you?'

'Neither the BCG nor the OEDCC are from the government, Mr Patten. We are both independently funded bodies, and we are willing to pay you a very generous sum to provide us with a list of words you feel should be cut from the English language,' Sparse sniffed.

'Why would *anyone* want to pay someone to make a list of words they don't like?'

'To protect the English language, of course!' Sparse cried. 'With every passing day new words are being invented, and we simply *don't have the room for it*. Our language isn't functional. If we want English to be a global language, we have to make some serious changes or else no one will be able to learn the bloody thing!' he said, with growing excitement. Perkins' cup was rattling in chorus. 'It's part of an initiative to strengthen our – ' he went silent suddenly. 'Well. I'm afraid I'm not at liberty to discuss this initiative, but let me assure you – *it is very secret and important and it shall restore Britannia to its former glory,*' he murmured.

'*You are mental,*' Colin hissed. 'Use your money for something else. Build a hospital or buy some schoolbooks or something. This is absurd.'

'Our research here at the Bureau of Complaints and Grievances has suggested that hospitals actually *encourage* illness, Mr Patten,' Sparse said gravely. 'Give people a place to go when they're sick, and they suddenly have all this incentive. No, this is a much better use of funds. And our funds are vast, sir. We can afford to pay you well,' he added, leaning forwards slightly.

Colin was confused, frightened and annoyed all at once. 'Who on earth is funding this bloody BG … BC … BFG of yours?' he demanded.

'Both the *BCG* and the OEDCC are privately funded,' Sparse sniffed, 'by a very important member of the English aristocracy. We are grateful for his patronage.'

'Well that makes sense, doesn't it,' Colin huffed. 'What, did he buy up all the guns and tweed he could and then decide he needed to waste a little more money?''

'I believe he is well-stocked in firearms and tweed, yes.'

'That was a bloody – oh, god,' he sighed deeply, resting his head in his palms.

'Come along, I'm sure you'll do fabulously! Now, there are plenty of words you must dislike, mmm?' he said encouragingly, picking up Colin's letter. 'You complained about quite a few here. I admit, I had to look *felicide* and *pingle* up, but I agree they are quite unnecessary.'

'Just stop.'

'Ah, and *soupçon*, you didn't enjoy, nor *resplendent*, or *egregious*, or … *highfalutin*. No, I'm afraid we might need that one,' Sparse murmured thoughtfully.

'Please. Stop. Now.'

'You see, the Bureau and the OEDCC are in the beginnings of a very promising relationship, Mr Patten. They have previously funded another one of our experiments with Perkins here,' Sparse said, slapping the large man on the back suddenly. Perkins didn't even blink, but he put down his macaroon. 'Although it didn't work as well as we'd hoped, I'm afraid. We only let him have fifty words to use in everyday life, like that parrot, and now he's gone mad,' he grimaced.

Colin looked at Perkins. 'He doesn't look mad.'

'I am,' Perkins nodded.

'I take it those are two of your allotted words?' he frowned.

'They are.'

'Well, we're up to four, now.'

'Conjugations don't count,' said Sparse.

'They don't,' Perkins agreed.

'Is the rule that he can only use two words at a time?'

'Enough play, Mr Patten,' Sparse interrupted crisply. 'Now, I would like you to think on our proposition and get back to us at your earliest convenience with a few sample suggestions.'

'Just – what – I mean – *no!*' Colin spluttered, standing up suddenly. '*No!* What, are you the language mafia? I've never heard of anything more ridiculous in my entire life!'

'Ha! There! Now, you could have said *existence*, couldn't you? But you chose the *shorter* word, the more economical one!' he said delightedly. 'Can't you see you're the perfect man for this task?'

A noise escaped from Colin's mouth, halfway between an exasperated sigh and a horrified whimper. 'God, you're in my head now!'

'It will be for the benefit of the whole English-speaking world, Mr Patten.'

'Please tell me my niece put you up to this? It was Caitlin, wasn't it?' he practically begged.

'Ah, yes, names are another issue entirely. All this Chandelier and Apple and Napkin nonsense is really getting quite out of hand,' Sparse said severely, nodding with Perkins.

'What, do you want to just kill off everyone with a name you don't like, huh?' Colin demanded wildly. 'What, just get rid of whatever you don't like, because their name doesn't *fit*?'

'Of course not, Mr Patten. We don't have the authority to assassinate,' he said crisply, in a tone that implied a loaded *yet*.

'I don't even understand what is happening anymore,' Colin murmured, shaking his head. 'No. Just *no*. You're mental; this is the most absurd thing I've ever heard of,' he insisted, rubbing his forehead to alleviate some of the intense pressure building up behind his eyes. 'It is *ridiculous*, it is *preposterous*, it is abso-freaking-lutely – '

'I'm not sure if our new, economical English can withstand tmesis, Mr Patten,' Sparse interrupted, causing Colin to groan loudly and turn straight to the door.

'Have an absolutely *resplendent* day, gentlemen,' he sneered, striding out into the hall without any clue of what had just happened in that conference room. 'Absolutely the most ridiculous waste of my – what a bloody – ' he muttered beneath his breath, marching back into the foyer.

'Leaving so soon, Mr Patten?' Maryanne greeted him brightly from behind the desk. The three miserable men were still at the settee, but they seemed to have changed positions and were now all sipping tea. He briefly wondered what sort of masquerade was waiting for them.

'Is this all a joke?' he asked her, a little desperately.

'I wish it were,' she huffed, suddenly speaking in a very American accent. But a moment later it was gone, and she fixed her smile back on straight. 'Well, have a lovely day, Mr Patten. I'm sorry the Bureau couldn't be of more assistance to you,' she said pleasantly.

Colin glanced over the three miserable men with a thoughtful frown, and then shook his head. He didn't really want to know if they were all just out-of-work actors or if the walls were made of cardboard or if Maryanne's smile was really painted on with lipstick and good customer service.

All he knew was that he was superlatively going to complain to someone about it.

A Time

Angela Collins

A watery brain;
an ineffable, breathing cloud-space.
Milk puddles dotting visions where
terrors,
pure and liquid,
moved their glass hand indelicately.
Silken fabric torn,
bloody,
seamless.

Partings

Julia Clark

You took me to a little lake below
the pines on which you'd floated your childhood
summers. It was an old friend's lake house, though
he was near strange to me then. But what would
we have said without his oblivion?
His cheerful effort to get to know and
reminisce simultaneously. Spun
atop an icy lake awaiting bands
of July warmth, we paused the plane we could
see coming. Paddling with a distaste
for wisdom, we hoped to hide in the woods
of our fir-tree memories, not wasting
time with true words. It could have happened to
anyone, but it was you – and me, too.

Fossils of the Stars

Brendan O'Shea

Fleets of tiny little probes combed through the farthest asteroid belts. Little lights on board were the only evidence of any kind of activity, flashing intermittently as they sampled the traces of iron lost in the void and calculated levels of oxygen now vanished. The fibre optics channelled information like blood throughout the wired systems of the probe's interior body. The sight of a small, polished sphere glinting with coloured lights was the kind that Lily would have loved to see. Her eyes would have gleamed with pleasure as she stretched her hands up to the windows as if to touch the stars.

'Daddy, look at the lights,' she might have said. He could remember the feel of her fingers curled firmly around his hand. Troughton couldn't bring himself to smile at the memory. She wasn't on that base, a metallic dome latching onto the side of the asteroid – at least not in a way she could stand beside him. She could never do that, not any more.

Something tugged at Troughton as he pressed his hand up to the glass window, feeling the grease. Perhaps it was melancholy. It seemed so strange, like a dream, that one tiny little probe had shorted out on this one asteroid just as it was floating back from the Alpha Centauri planetary systems with rock samples. A survey team had been sent up in an old tin rocket to take a look because of one cursory scan from a satellite. There was something metallic there, but that was the strangest thing. It wasn't like a vein of metal, threaded through the rock of the asteroid. A paleontological survey wouldn't be sent out after that sort of thing; a Jupiter mining vessel would have sufficed, grabbing the asteroid with claw-like appendages and grinding it down in the circular maw of its refinery. No, this metal was galvanised in some way; an alloy. The metal seemed more artificial, less natural. Something constructed was lost in the rock.

He sat there, waiting. Lily not so much watched but felt the little lights flickering on the screens, lighting up like a Christmas tree whenever anything metallic reached their little mining robot's range. Troughton wasn't sure how it felt to her. Maybe it felt like raindrops falling on bare skin, something cold and wet that reminds you that you can feel the world. It could just as easily have been like a needle-prick. It was an experience he could never have. He could never know what it felt like for Lily to live as she was.

Maybe it would all come to nothing, the metal locked inside the rock of the asteroid. Perhaps it was just a crashed satellite: with hundreds upon millions of probes combing the universe for the faintest blips of anything, it was always a possibility that one had crashed somewhere unnoticed. Whatever it was remained locked within the rock like a fossil, waiting for man to peel back the surface and birth it out of the asteroid that imprisoned it.

'Just what are you?' he asked himself, taking in the smell of fuel and rock as he breathed in deeply. There was something hypnotic about that smell, mixed together in his mind to create something so industrial. He could almost feel his mind slowing, his heart feeling less pained thinking of Lily stuck watching the lights.

Taking his hand away from the window and wiping the grease on his dark jacket, Troughton walked down the corridor to the main room, footsteps echoing cyclically in his ears. Absently he brushed his hand over his breast pocket, feeling the edges of the fob watch tucked away inside. How times had changed indeed. His mind's eye saw through the forgotten dust of history to Cope and Marsh who stared vacantly back, their eyes long dead in the pits of their bitter rivalry. They stood on the fields of bones that they'd unearthed with such vigorous enthusiasm. Under their pick and shovel they'd turned America over, extracting from the earth the lost traces of creatures dead since before man first climbed down from the trees. Troughton felt an irresistible notion turning in his head. Whatever was trapped within the asteroid would mean just as much to him as those bones had meant to those two men who were now long gone.

'Professor, we're about to get visual,' spoke a voice – Lily's voice – crackled by radio interference. It was a young voice, a soft voice, pronouncing each word with such clarity it betrayed her unfamiliarity with the sounds. It echoed off the metal and the rock like the ghost's voice that it was.

There was something eerie about hearing Lily's distorted voice ringing in the carved corridors of that asteroid base. It was one thing to stand on the earth, that tiny little world falling through space, and hear the voice of another human, especially a child. Standing on an asteroid lost in the depths of space with just a small team of palaeontologists, Troughton felt it burning in his mouth. It was like walking in void. It was the loneliness of it all, Troughton supposed; the knowledge that those people were the only ones living and breathing, all except for Lily.

For a flicker of a moment he wondered if that was how the men scavenging the badlands of the earth felt, lost amongst hills searching for fossilised rock in the red dust. Those men had never sat by her bedside though, watching her as she swallowed stories of animals lost to the rock and buried by the fires of an asteroid strike with such fascination.

'Will I ever find some dinosaur bones, daddy?' she had asked, looking up at him and hanging off his silence. Troughton could only remember smiling whenever she asked, then ruffling her soft brown hair and smiling as she smiled, lingering only until her eyes had closed. Something fell down Troughton's cheek, something long and thin and wet. It couldn't be a tear.

'I repeat, Professor Troughton, we're about to get visual.'

He reached the door, a large yellow bulkhead which, like much of the base, had been cannibalised from the rickety old crate of a rocket that had propelled them so far. Streaks of paint, shorn off from age, revealed the dull steel from which it was constructed. Troughton craned his head towards a lowered microphone and whistled into it. The tune was old, very old. It was the tune of lights flashing as spaceships lowered, blasting out a rumbling reply with the brass severity of a tuba as a man stood on a platform pressing keys on a keyboard. The door wheezed and pulled itself up and

Troughton squinted through the exhaust fumes. Just beyond the door were screens, glinting planes of glass wrapped around the walls of a cavern peering into the eyes of a small mining robot.

'How much longer until we have a visual do you think, Lily?' Troughton asked, his voice gentle, as he looked around the room. There was nobody standing out there with him. Of course they were back on the ship, pulling out their cases and equipment to unearth the metal thing trapped inside. Someone was going to want to see the samples.

A smile tugged at his mouth: the further humanity fanned across the stars and the larger the empire became, the more anxious they seemed to be to have something tactile there before them. They wanted something that they could touch, as if touching meant that they knew it and understood it. Perhaps it was just the need for proof that there was something, even if nobody ever knew what it was. As long as they knew that something had been there, that was enough.

'Calculations indicate we'll have a visual in less than ninety seconds,' Lily replied, the voice still cracked by interference. Troughton smiled as he saw a line on the screen undulate as Lily spoke. Perhaps one day Lily would stand before him again, incarnate. Perhaps one day he'd be able to look into her eyes and see something of himself reflected there. At least he had her voice, but at times even that wasn't enough to pull his heart from the depths of melancholy or his thoughts from dwelling on the nights he'd spent reading to her. 'Professor, should I begin the countdown?'

He walked up to the screen, feeling the light as it emanated against his worn features. The computer hummed as Troughton watched the almost motionless line. Being so close to the screen he could see the faint twitch of activity. He breathed in calmly. The line was almost like a mouth, only noticeably moving when Lily spoke. Vaguely he recalled something about faces and the ability to recognise something human in even the simplest representation of eyes and a mouth. A line was a simple mouth.

As Lily waited in silence, Troughton could almost see the shape of her mouth as she looked up and smiled at him. Staring at his hand he could feel the softness of her hair as he brushed loose strands out of her eyes. There was something in the way she looked up at him with those eyes, bright and wide and smiling as she clung to the stuffed dinosaur in her arms.

'Can we find some dinosaurs today? You promised daddy, you promised!'

Looking at the blue glow of the screen, it was only now he really noticed how warm and pink her cheeks had been back then. He could recall how she bounced on her feet, smiling with her teeth in that childlike way, thrusting her toy as close to his face as she could. There was no bounce in her step and no toothy smile looking up at him now.

He touched the screen as if it was her cheek, but as Troughton felt the plastic that was fuzzy with static he realised that this was her cheek now, just as the line was her smile now. The thought echoed in his mind that he shouldn't have to look at Lily's echo, trapped as a computer. No father should.

Closing his eyes he could see Lily, the line on the screen, flaring into an orange inferno that cracked the sky like a fissure. Troughton could feel the wisps of grass cutting against his hands like paper. He tried screaming as tears split his ash-coated face. He could only choke. The sky of fire was cracked apart by the shockwave of an explosion, black smoke falling to the ground. Troughton turned, fingers trembling, as he looked for Lily. As he crawled closer to Lily he felt his eyes struggling as he succumbed to the drug-like trance of the heavy layer of smoke.

He had held her hand and noticed how limp it felt. The arm was dead. He had remembered this again when he stared into his dust-stained hands while the instruments of surgery carved through Lily's bone and careful hands slid out the grey muscle within. Troughton just stared at his hands that were coated in dirt, imagining the cracks to be dead valleys. They were nothing more than canyons lost in a lattice of badlands. It was all he could do at the time to stop himself from imagining just what kind of pain Lily had been in. His eyes were now red with tears and his throat burned as he tried to look at that line again as what it was – just a line, only undulating when Lily spoke.

Grinding his teeth, Troughton continued to stare at the line. It was impossible to look away. He wasn't sure how he'd feel if Lily began to speak again, if the line flickered and he wasn't watching. He tried not to imagine the wires pinned into Lily's brain, linking her to all of this. Troughton clenched his fist. She wouldn't be a shelled ghost forever.

'That's okay Lily, we don't need a countdown,' he said in answer to her question. He could feel it in his eyes and in the back of his dry throat as he choked out the words. 'We don't want to be that cliché. Just tell me when the robot breaks through.'

For just a moment he found himself running his worn thumb over the dull metal casing of his watch, feeling the warmth emanating within. No, this was enough cliché for him. As he stared at the metal, recalling the sound of ticking gears and eyes blinded by a cascade of white light, the thought of digging in red earth didn't seem so obscure. If he clicked open the watch, held the badlands and the faces of Cope and Marsh in his eyes, perhaps he'd feel the breeze on his skin and stare up at the sunlight for the first time since he'd left earth for this asteroid.

He could lie in dry grass, watching the shapes of the clouds and imagine just for a moment what it would be like to have Lily beside him, maybe eating an ice cream and wearing that hooded jacket she always used to wear. Troughton swallowed thoughts and stared at the line. The line was Lily now. That was all she was; a voice echoing in an isolated asteroid falling through space. Troughton watched as a robot appeared on the screen, tearing through the rock with powerful metal claws. He almost asked Lily to call the palaeontologists to witness as this creature was birthed from this desolate little rock. But they'd never have come. As the robot clawed through the last layer, revealing the metallic features of a face, Troughton alone stood and watched; his only company was the sound of humming machines.

Korean Food, Room for Rent

Blythe S Worthy

Veronica stood smoking on the stoop of George's Kebabs and thought about all the men she could have fucked, flicking through her memory on an infinite rolodex of dicks. She could hear George counting change out into the tills inside, stopping every now and then to serve someone. His overly kind tone and easy laugh made her teeth grind. She squeezed her eyes shut.

Lano, who was tall and thin. She met him at a party and he talked about her nice legs, pressed his cold nose against her ear and 'AHHH-d' an orgasm into his own jeans.

Paul, who was a thick, stout Turkish man who worked in the kebab shop when she was fifteen. His thick, stout fingers strained against the fat plastic gloves that drowned her own hands.

Brad, who was a family friend eight years her senior. He let her lie on his bed and watch films with him when she was seventeen. She pretended not to know her shirt was riding up over her hips, angling over her low-slung pants like pale, uncooked cake mix.

Ben, who used to follow her around at parties in high school, offering to massage her shoulders and back because she 'looked tense'.

The nice Indian taxi driver once asked her to recall her first romantic memory.

How many could have reached in, pressed up against her chest and dug around until they found something in her that made them explode?

Gasps in her ear and sweaty chests stuck together making sucking sounds as they pulled apart?

Maybe she could have had a continual merry-go-round of squeezes coming into her room like her housemate, inviting anyone who came across her path old enough to maintain some semblance of body hair.

Maybe they could have grabbed her hips, moaning and grunting as they pushed the boredom out of her until she collapsed, full of lust and content.

Veronica groaned and leaned her head back as she exhaled a great cloud of smoke into the cobwebs over her head, rhythmically tapping out a tattoo onto the step with her heel in time with the pounding in her head.

She checked her watch, sniffed, and wiped away the drips on the end of her nose with the back of her hand. Stared at the snail tracks of mucus it made across her knuckles. Smelled the smoke on her fingers. Bit the burnt scab on her thumb that still hadn't fully healed. Dragged her nails through her scalp irritably and came out with short black strands of hair caught in the manicure.

Stared at the blue neon sign blinking at her from across the street: *KOREAN FOOD* it proclaimed, with a curved arrow pointing to three blacked out windows, and underneath: *Room For Rent.*

Saw George's face when she had come into work with her new short hair. An inky black, his frown of distaste.

'Whaddya done that for? You look like onea them fahhking goth lesbos.'

She hacked out a cough and squatted, stretching out her thigh muscles. She'd been standing at the grill all day; her shift heading into the dinner rush.

She was hoping to finish before the girls snapping gum and calling people on their phones in sequined shorts leaned over the counter and asked questions about George's day as they eyed the $4 pizza in the window. They waited for boyfriends, then moved on or sat for chips and kebabs, beer bellies grumbling.

George would always pay these ones special attention, smiling greedily, trying to make them laugh, pointing at the shop's sign when he snagged their name, proclaiming 'This is MY shop! I'M George!'

To which the girls always laughed, looking around in amusement, meeting eyes with Veronica and hastily looking away.

Clomping out in shoes that weighed more than them as four a.m. came and went.

Veronica stood in her dowdy George's Kebabs shirt, her nonna apron bunched up, and hated him. She remembered George in his pristine Parramatta flat, stomach pressed up against hers as their drunken breath intermingled.

Because he was her boss and because she didn't care if he thought she was fat.

She remembered the rash and pain that grew with her regret, day after day until she waddled to hospital and shook someone's hand for telling her she couldn't have sex with anyone until she told them she had hepatitis B.

The rolodex goes around in her head and always lands on George, slinging his slack stomach over his jeans, trying to pretend it doesn't exist.

Thinking of all the women he's going to fuck.

The Runner

DL Keenan

Out to the East purple clouds were brewing on the horizon and the wild Tasman bellowed and roared beneath. The sky above the clouds was clear, and the deep purple of the clouds met a slide of pastel from pink to orange all the way through to blue overhead. The ocean made its way to the coast through jagged spears of rock, rising from the depths of the water. Further in, the movement of waves had taken its toll on the rocky seabed breaking it up and smoothing out all the broken pieces and shells. The short beach was surrounded by small cliffs, with a set of stairs carved into the rock on one side. The shore itself was made up of smooth pebbles and shells and the occasional fishing sinker, but no sand. Sometimes a fisherman would leave guts, or scales, or bones from the day's spoils. Fishermen stood on the rocks at the foot of the cliffs near the beach – old men, all of them, smoking cigars and quarreling about the catches of their youth. In the last moments of sundown the light in the little valley was muted and no shadows could be found, while the skies above exploded with dark, beautiful colours. In the mornings it was different; the sun was thrown from the sea and the valley was illuminated with bright, gentle light, caressing the smooth pebbles and bouncing off the cliff walls, greeting the early-morning fishermen. Along the top of the ever-rising cliff ran a track of old cement, well-walked by many generations. The track was connected on either side to a string of beaches and seaside towns with cozy little shops and people who knew each other on a first-name basis.

* * *

Eventually, you go numb and enter a kind of Zen state, lost in your own thoughts and at one with the pavement ahead of you. That's the good part. In fact, it's the only good reason I can think of.

* * *

Slowly I made my way up the hill, laboured breaths painfully spat out at uneven intervals. Each step forward was a testament of will, an action that required every ounce of concentration imaginable, mostly just to keep the thoughts of giving up from the front of my mind. Slowly, from the dull thud of rubber, a rhythm began to form and match the painful breath. My lungs burnt like embers in my chest, heating my stomach and stinging my throat. I looked down to my feet, then back up to the path ahead, my eyes darting back and forth to distract myself from the torture. That's really what it was in the end, torture. I didn't want to do it, but I couldn't let myself stop. I was being moved by something inside me and had nothing say in the matter. I felt my head getting lighter, like always, my back straightened, and then nothing. It's meditative, therapeutic even; a state without any feeling. A state confined to thoughts, where you're pushed in and forced to swim around in them, however murky the waters may be.

Screw coach, I thought to myself, that son of a bitch, who is he to tell me he never missed a training his whole career, what a load that was, telling me that *I'm* the one not trying, as if the rest of the goddamned team were gods among us; how grateful we should all be to be graced by their presence. Screw them all. The way they all walked with their lungs full, puffing out their chests, a little dip in their step. I never did get along with them and I guess that's why I couldn't do it in the end – keep playing that is. I always struggled to understand them; I could never get into the mindset, I just couldn't make myself care. For all of them, it was more than a game; it was a way of life. It was a creed that made them honourable and respectable men of society and once they were done with that season they would pick up an oar and then quest for prestige would continue. Before the games someone would yell a speech about 'men never backing down' and the coming 'battle', but for me it was always just going to be a group of boys playing around in the grass. There wasn't any honour in it, it was just something to do. Between the schools it didn't seem to matter though; they hated each other, and rivalries that had been around for fifty years persisted in even the youngest boys – it had been ingrained into them at a young age. The gold embroidery below their pockets brought them great authority. It could have said anything though, 'Firsts Janitors'. I spat a laugh in between breaths. I could have thought of something wittier but this was not the time for wit.

Out in the distance the purple clouds had matured to a dark blue, and I could just make out the grey blur of rain when I managed to turn my head. I ran forward, struggling up the hill and noticed two girls appear from behind bushes at the bottom of the stairs. They seemed young, about twenty years old, and looked to be impersonating athletes. Between the dim words and high-pitched giggles of their conversation rose plumes of smoke from the cigarettes they sucked on. Head to toe they were covered in the top-of-the-line sportswear. They were so heavily lathered in makeup their faces were almost indistinguishable from one another. Both of them had bleached blonde hair and an orange face, clothed in the same tight-fitting running shorts. The only real feature of distinction between them was that the girl on the right was a slightly darker shade of orange than her friend. Don't get me wrong – they were good looking – but in the worst kind of way, the kind of way that makes you hate yourself for being attracted to them, fooled by their cheap tricks. Like pushing a bruise you can't stop yourself looking at them, but god it isn't what I want to do. I wondered if they were aware of the hypocrisy, for all I knew they were but they didn't look it. They could have been PhD candidates in metaphysics though; I wouldn't have known any different. Would that have made a difference? Maybe, but an uninteresting mind can so easily be disguised by reading. Boring people regurgitating beautifully intricate ideas that aren't their own, tricking everyone around them: I know I do it. Still, it ate at me to be attracted to them. As I passed I tasted the cigarette smoke in the back of my throat. It made me feel nauseous, the one on the left pointed at me, flared her nostrils and laughed. I was glad.

I pushed the girls back into the furthest regions of my mind and tried to focus on whatever else I could – pain, even – but it wouldn't work, the delirium stopped me. The rock that signalled the four-kilometre mark slowly bobbed past me. Halfway had come and gone. I didn't care much but longed for the hill-climb to be over: the last was always the worst. I knew they were coming, the thirteen sets of stairs that led to the park atop the hill. Every time I did the run, I counted the stairs as best I could, the numbers falling from my lips as I let air escape. The first five sets were bigger than the following eight, so it was always crushing to hear 'five', knowing that eight sets still lay ahead you while your body told you to give up and quit. The climb itself was always a blur of pain and this time was no different. Before I knew it the earth of the park came into view. I could hear children's laughter and the deep buzz of engines carried on the wind. I was falling back into reality, back in to my aching body.

I briefly stopped to a join a queue of dogs waiting for the tap. Sweat dripped from my brow into my eye, the salty water burning it. I became aware of the way my tongue stuck to my throat and my feet began carrying my weight again; my vision darkened and light spots swirled in the sky. My shirt began to shrink around my neck, chocking me. I tore it from my back and dropped it on the grass. I needed water. One of the dogs came by and sniffed at the shirt, looking up at me before its owner came over and yelled at it to 'leave that man alone Jackson!' I pulled the water into my mouth, letting it cool me before spitting it out. After a few spits I allowed myself to swallow a small gulp and felt the cool liquid slip down my throat and into the top of my stomach. I felt relieved, I felt as if I could breathe again. I picked up my shirt and drifted over to a particularly comfortable looking patch of grass and planted myself there, my head still spinning. I shut my eyes.

A small, delicate park graced the top of the hill I had just climbed. On one side it was bordered by road, on another a steep grassy hill and stairs and finally a fifty-metre drop straight down to the rocks and waves below. Atop the cliff was a flimsy wooden fence to keep the inattentive away. The view over the cliff filled me with the most primal sense of panic as I stared down into an abyss, engulfed in nature's terrifying embrace. Powerful swells crashed against the smooth rocks at the base of the cliff, worn down by the centuries of abuse. All the while, fishing birds gracefully negotiated the waves and rocks, diving underneath the swells only to burst forth at the very last moment with a beak full of sea creatures. The bird's dance with death saved its own life, but in the same motion took with it the life of another. I tried to think of where they must sleep – the birds that is. All I could come up with was that the flock must sleep as it glides through the night sky, travelling for hours at a time over huge expanses of empty sea, stopping only at sunrise and sunset to steal the ocean's treasures, before continuing their endless journey. Perhaps they took turns sleeping to make sure their course was true. I knew this wasn't the case, but wished it with all of my heart.

Small rolling hills discouraged people from venturing too close to the edge of the cliff and tall pine trees threw useless shadows through the park at midday, too small to offer refuge. Scattered between the tall pines, towards the edge were ancient tea-trees as thick as a man, all bent over and horrifically distorted. The scent was intoxicating though, and as it rose up my nostrils I could feel my muscles relax and I couldn't help but sigh. It was the sort of park that only beautiful light fills, and you feel a strange sense of intimacy with it. It creates the warm, sepia-toned memories of your childhood, even if you only see it as an adult. Long dark shadows leak from the people in it as sun lowers – only they never notice; I think I might be the only one that does. On the other side of the park life continued: little kids chased dogs and one another and adults talked in little groups ignoring everything around them. They looked like the sort to be discussing the state of the economy or the new car they wanted. None of them seemed to notice the symphony of light and shadows at their feet, or the delicate dance of the birds. Not a single one stopped to look at anything. They just were. I envied them. They were allowed to sleep, while I was forced to keep the course true, the navigator always on watch. I stared at everything around me trying to take in as much as I could of the fleeting light.

The night sky was starting to take over and there was a change in the wind, colder and more violent. It was time to move on. I clambered back to my feet and walked over to the other side of the park as the remaining two people left through a gate to the road. A few small sets of stairs carried me back down to the path along the cliff and I forced my walk into a run. When you first start it usually takes a few hundred metres for the pain to start, a little bit of time to run arrogantly, faster than you know you should. This time I was beaten before I even began. Straightaway it felt like I was choking, the laboured breath returning quickly. The muscles in my legs tightened and my strides shortened even further; people could have walked past me easily. I pushed my mind back to Coach, or the girls or even the birds, but they weren't places my mind wanted to go. As soon as I thought I had it the pain put away somewhere it would bounce right back and prove to me how little left I had. I gave up trying and left my mind to its own devices, free to scurry to whichever dark corner it pleased. I only got glimpses of where it went through the pain. At one stage I saw an afternoon coated in gold, down by a river with a boat and some fishing rods. Or maybe it wasn't that at all, maybe it was the pontoon of the rowing shed, with the boys taking out the boats before the morning's race. I couldn't be sure. Then I was back on the path, wading through the gloom. The sea was worse now; an old fishing boat with a yellow light on in the cabin was taking a beating, being thrown up and down on the swells like I was on the cliffs. We were both alone, left to keep watch on the journey. The flashes of memories became less distinct and frequent.

I couldn't do it anymore, there wasn't anywhere for me to escape to. My mind had been used up over the last six kilometres, I had nothing left in it, stuck in my aching body. It was agony all the way from the muscles in the bottom of my feet to the ache in my forehead. I couldn't back down though, as I came closer to the end I heard the thumps of rubber getting closer together, faster and faster. I couldn't control my breathing now, it was beyond me, retching and gasping and I pulled together one final effort, moving myself faster and faster. I was proud. To someone else I imagine I would have looked terrible, back hunched, with short steps and a rolling head breathing so loudly I could be heard from twenty metres away, but there wasn't much I could do about that.

* * *

Out West the last drops of sunlight fled to illuminate some undiscovered part of the world and left me drenched in the florescence of streetlights.

The Party

Andrew Lee

'Nick! It's Nick everyone!'

Jillian explodes out of a knot of people and jumps on him, almost knocking the bottle from his hands. She pulls his neck down to hug him and he winces, gets a mouthful of hair and plastic leaves.

'You *came*! You actually came to something for once!'

She's going to bring up how late he is. He overshot the house by a dozen stops on the bus and had to stump back through Marrickville's sidestreets, the late-summer night panting out humidity. Walking in it for half an hour was enough to soak him in his own sweat. He's barely in the door and already he can smell himself, feel his shirt clinging rankly to his back. Jillian lets go and looks him up and down, her mouth making a cartoonish 'O' of outrage.

'You're not in *theme*! I *hate* you!' She beats on his chest with little fists.

He didn't dress in theme because, Jesus, you give four day's notice for your fucking house party and expect people to come in theme? *A Midsummer Night's Dream*, was that it?

'And you're late! You're' – she pokes him with a painted nail – 'a bad *person*.'

'No I'm not,' he says, grinning, teasing. 'I just don't like you very much.'

'*Nick*! You're *mean*.' Jillian's breasts press deliberately into his chest as she hugs him again. Her boyfriend's here somewhere but Jillian only knows how to flirt with men or ignore them completely. Nick graduated from the latter category almost a year ago and has missed it ever since.

He does the rounds – backslaps, cheeks kissed, how are you, how's uni, how's work – before finding a spot on a low couch in a corner of the lounge room and getting to work on his bottle. Ten minutes later he's beginning to feel better. He sinks into the couch and drinks the wine and splays his legs out like a drunk uncle at a Christmas party. He watches a crack on the wall for a little bit.

The couch cushion rises under him – it doesn't click that someone's sat down next to him right away. A too-hard clap on the shoulder brings him back.

'Nick, mate! Good to see ya!'

Oh god, it's Jillian's new one, the college boy. They've only met twice before and already Nick hates him with the special intensity he reserves for all men in polo shirts. What's his name again? Jayden or Lachlan or some fucking thing like that.

'How *are* ya, mate? How's life?'

Jesus, stop calling me mate. Who calls people mate?

'I'm good, yeah. You?'

'*Yeah* mate, not bad, I've just started work at this law firm actually, friend of my dad's –'

That was easy. Nick rests his head on the back of the couch and lifts the lightening bottle. His mouth snarls around the burn of the wine. On the far side of the room a clutch of girls huddle around a punchbowl. He dimly realises that he'd like to have sex with one of them, the same way he'd like to one day learn how to play guitar. He isn't really sure which of the girls, though.

'… Nick? What do you reckon?'

Polo Shirt's looking at him a little cross-eyed, wondering whether to be offended. Hell, let him be. He could probably talk his way out of it, but this idiot isn't worth it.

'No idea, man. Wouldn't have a clue.' He drains the bottle and holds it aloft by the neck, sweeps it in a grand arc like a prophet's staff.

'Wouldn't have a fucking clue!'

An awkward silence falls. Nick dives into it, lets it swallow him. Polo Shirt suddenly looks like a homeless guy on the bus. He clears his throat and looks towards Jillian for help, but she's joined the punchbowl girls and has nothing on her mind but getting pissed enough to brag about the hangover. Finally, Nick lets him off the hook.

'Won't be a sec, I'm gonna grab a beer.'

'No problem mate, no problem! I'll catch you up later!'

He leaves Jillian's boy on the couch with his relief and heads toward the kitchen. The speakers have been set up on top of the fridge to stop people messing with the playlist, turning the kitchen into a standard sharehouse dancefloor. Nick threads his way through a crowd of messy, heaving kids, dripping sweat and screaming half-remembered OutKast lyrics at each other. Someone spills cider on his arm and he doesn't have the grace not to give the guy a shove.

He scowls into the fridge, wondering what to steal. He should've anticipated this: Jillian hated beer and never bought it for her own dos. Eventually he plucks a Boags from its cardboard cradle. Polo Shirt was drinking Boags. He shuts the door and leans against the fridge, eyes shut, the speakers thrumming a tattoo into his brain stem.

Someone taps him on the shoulder. He tenses, ready to defend his beer, but it's only a friend of Jillian's he's seen out a few times, Adam something. He's a quiet, skinny-shouldered guy, and something in his face always reminds Nick of a sad old painting, caked over with dust. He has the solemn look of the very drunk. He leans in and shouts over the music.

'Come outside, I need a smoke.'

Nick doesn't smoke, but he makes an exception this time without quite knowing why. He and Adam have done a lot of drinking in groups together, but they only know each other in the slightly wary way of people with many mutual acquaintances. Conversation with such people is dangerous – it can expose to the both of you how little you have in common. He nods, though. He needs a breather.

'You want a drink?'

'Yeah, what are you having?'

'A Boags, I'll grab you one.'

They escape the suffocation of the kitchen, squeezing past the dancers to the back door, and set up on the veranda outside. Adam passes him a cigarette and lighter and he shuts his eyes tight as he lights up to keep the smoke out of his eyes. The backyard smells of heat and rotting fruit, jacaranda blossoms and passionfruit vines. The night is thick with the promise of rain. They sit for a while, cooling down, letting the smoke leave them.

'Saw you talking to Damon.'

That's it, Damon, that's Polo Shirt's name. Who names their kid Damon? He never stood a chance.

'Yeah, he's a nice guy.'

'He's a prick.' Adam's grin is too wide for humour. There is something in his voice, some careful absence that Nick recognises. He sits hunched over, rolling the bottle in his palms. Nick runs his tongue along the knife edge of his teeth, tasting the remnants of the wine, feeling the outline of the question he is meant to ask, the one that will crack Adam open.

'How are you and Steph?' He knows how they are. The last time he saw Adam was in a corner booth on the second floor of Zanzibar, his face hidden behind the curtain of her hair. That was two weeks ago – now Steph's at the other end of the house with the punchbowl girls and Adam's out here with a vague acquaintance and a stolen Boags. For a while he doesn't say anything, he runs his hands through his crinkly black hair.

'I dunno man, we've seen each other a few times and, and I thought things were going really well but I don't know if, I don't think she … '

Nick doesn't look at him, stares out at the dark garden and draws on his cigarette. It pleases him a little that he has learned to do this without coughing. A plane comes shrieking in from the north, lights blinking with car-crash urgency. He watches it go.

'I dunno, I just … ' Adam wars against the faint quake in his voice. For a moment his glasses go cloudy as the eyes behind them look into something bottomless.

'I just want to *hold* her, y'know? I just want to but I *can't*, and it's, it's … '

Nick gazes at his hands. People often do this with him, pour their weaknesses into his silence. It is a very difficult thing for a young man to admit his humiliation to another but something about his manner invites it, promises a kind of stoic consolation. He has learned over many nights like this the words that will console and the words that will devastate.

Above them, above everything, great broad-backed clouds that blew west and broke on the mountains are marching back to the coast, unfurling their long banners of rain. It falls now, finally, crackling off tin rooftops, making fireflies of the streetlights. Down the street an ancient Greek couple murmur at the sound and turn over in their sleep.

His hand on Adam's bucking shoulder, Nick sits on the veranda watching the rain come quietly down. Behind them 'Gold Digger' comes on, and people scream and run to dance in the kitchen.

Jesus, he thinks. I am so tired of this.